The Person of the Therapist Training M

The Person of the Therapist Training Model presents a model that prepares therapists to make active and purposeful use of who they are, personally and professionally, in all aspects of the therapeutic process—relationship, assessment and intervention. The authors take a process that seems vague and elusive, the self-of-the-therapist work, and provide a step-by-step description of how to conceptualize, structure and implement a training program designed to facilitate the development of effective therapists, who are skilled at using their whole selves in their encounters with clients. This book looks to make conscious and planned use of a therapist's race, gender, culture, values, life experience, and in particular, personal vulnerabilities and struggles in how he or she relates to and works with clients. This evidence-supported resource is ideal for clinicians, supervisors and training programs.

Harry J. Aponte, MSW, LCSW, LMFT, HPhD, is a Clinical Associate Professor in the Couple and Family Therapy Department at Drexel University.

Karni Kissil, PhD, LMFT, has 20 years of experience as a clinician, working with individuals, couples and families in diverse practice settings. She is currently in private practice in Florida.

The Person of the Therapist Training Model
Mastering the Use of Self

**Edited by Harry J. Aponte
and Karni Kissil**

Routledge
Taylor & Francis Group

NEW YORK AND LONDON

First published 2016
by Routledge
711 Third Avenue, New York, NY 10017

and by Routledge
2 Park Square, Milton Park, Abingdon, Oxon, OX14 4RN

Routledge is an imprint of the Taylor & Francis Group, an informa business

Library of Congress Cataloging-in-Publication Data
Names: Aponte, Harry J., editor. | Kissil, Karni, editor.
Title: The person of the therapist training model : mastering the use of self / edited by Harry J. Aponte and Karni Kissil.
Description: New York, NY : Routledge, 2016. | Includes bibliographical references and index.
Identifiers: LCCN 2015026625 | ISBN 9781138856905 (hbk, alk. paper) | ISBN 9781138856912 (pbk, alk. paper) | ISBN 9781315719030 (ebk)
Subjects: | MESH: Psychotherapy—education. | Counseling—education.
Classification: LCC RC480 | NLM WM 18 | DDC 616.89/140071—dc 3
LC record available at http://lccn.loc.gov/2015026625

ISBN: 978-1-138-85690-5 (hbk)
ISBN: 978-1-138-85691-2 (pbk)
ISBN: 978-1-315-71903-0 (ebk)

Typeset in Baskerville
by Keystroke, Station Road, Codsall, Wolverhampton

Printed and bound in the United States of America by Publishers Graphics, LLC on sustainably sourced paper.

To my beloved wife, Theresa, and my darling daughter, Maria. —H.A.

Contents

Contributors

Editors

Harry J. Aponte, MSW, LCSW, LMFT, HPhD, Clinical Associate Professor in the Couple and Family Therapy Department at Drexel University, USA.

I'm much influenced by my psychoanalytic background and structural family therapy, but take an integrative approach to therapy. My belief in and sensitivity to how our flawed humanity contributes to our empathy as therapists has helped lead me to the Person-of-the-Therapist (POTT) model.

Karni Kissil, PhD, licensed marriage and family therapist in private practice in Jupiter, Florida.

Living in two different cultures and having been trained in two different therapeutic modalities (psychodynamic and family therapy) help me think outside the box as a therapist. I like the POTT model because of its emphasis on self-acceptance of our flawed humanity. It allows me to sit more comfortably in my own skin and as a result have more freedom in my clinical work.

Contributors

Renata Carneiro, MS PhD.

My culture, background in theater, and family helped me to always be curious about others. My preferred theoretical orientation is Narrative Family Therapy. I enjoy working with clients who are different from me, and learn about their experiences. The experiential component of POTT appeals to me because I can use all parts of myself to connect with clients.

Christian Jordal, PhD, LMFT, Clinical Assistant Professor and Associate Director of the Master's Degree program in Couple and Family Therapy at Drexel University, USA.

I use a variety of approaches with my clients, depending on the presenting issues. I have advanced training in couple and sex therapies. I am drawn to the POTT model because I believe clinicians must understand who we are as people, to understand who we are as practitioners.

Alba Niño, PhD, LCMFT, Assistant Professor in Couple and Family Therapy Programs at Alliant International University, San Diego, USA.

My clinical work is informed by attachment and emotion centered therapies. My current research interests include immigrant therapists, cross-cultural therapeutic relationships and effective ways to train therapists. The POTT training has become central in my work as a researcher and as a professor. POTT's philosophy and assignments help trainees humanize themselves, their clients and the profession of psychotherapy.

Jody Russon, MA, PhD, Postdoctoral Fellow at Drexel University, USA.

As a family therapist and researcher, my interests are centered around attachment-informed interventions and socio-ecological perspectives on gender and sexual identity. The POTT process of using my own experiences to empathize with families allows me to continue seeking my fullest potential as therapist. As a wounded healer, I gain the ability to reach out to others from a place of emotional wisdom and openness.

Senem Zeytinoglu, PhD, family therapist at Kozyatağı Acıbadem Hospital Department of Pediatric Neurosurgery and Clinical Supervisor at İstanbul Bilgi University Couple and Family Therapy Program, Turkey.

Having the ability to use my own life experiences grounds me when working with people from different paths of life than mine. I work systemically; have extensive training in emotionally focused therapy and EMDR. POTT is my tool to use my emotions, beliefs and biases for the benefit of my clients.

Preface

Our Stories

Harry J. Aponte

My development of the POTT model has both personal and professional roots. One year out of graduate school in my native New York, and as a son of Puerto Rican parents, I travelled to what seemed to me to be the land of Oz, commonly known as Kansas, for a year of postgraduate training at the Menninger Clinic, only to remain for another seven years on staff. The patients and their families were mostly well-to-do Anglo-Saxon people who culturally were foreign to me. Yet, I was charged with working with the patients' families, which meant I had to learn to relate to them, understand them and somehow be of help to them. For me the socio-cultural differences presented a significant challenge to communication and emotional resonance. However, in this bastion of psychoanalysis I was also learning about countertransference, a concept that spoke to what our own life experience brings to our reactions to client issues and psychological histories. It fostered self-reflection about what I brought to the understanding and relationship with patients and clients. I became aware that it was not only of how my ethnic roots and low socioeconomic background related to work; it was also my closely held history of a troubled family life that contributed to my reticence about my personal life, and to my proneness to self-sufficiency. I entered psychoanalysis at Menninger's—something meant to help resolve our personal issues, Freud's answer to preventing therapists' issues from contaminating the therapy we did. I learned to self-reflect and to be self-aware, but certainly did not come to any root resolution of the core issues I carried with me from my past. However, I discovered in those years in Topeka, Kansas, how to open and stretch myself to relate to the common humanity of the people with whom I worked, however different they were from me. The acceptance of the reality of our common human frailties helped me to unlock the doors to our common life struggles.

Fast forward, after my stint at Menninger's I was invited by Salvador Minuchin to join him at the Philadelphia Child Guidance Clinic in Philadelphia that was working on and researching the use of family therapy with disadvantaged families. These were my people, and I would have little trouble relating to their life experiences. However, while the psychoanalytic perspective focused on our early childhood experiences, the Child Guidance's structural family therapy orientation focused on the immediate experience in the present actuality of the therapy room—among family members and between therapist and family. While my psychoanalytic experience helped me to self-reflect, and motivated me to self-correct, here in the immediacy of the face-to-face encounter with families, I had to maneuver through what was going on right now between the families and myself, which was not only a professional process, but also something quite personal. There would be no time to "fix" my flaws. I would need to work with and through all that I brought to the therapeutic process to enhance, enrich and potentiate the effectiveness of my work. I was connecting my professional performance to my personal life experience—past but also what was evolving for me personally at the moment in my interactions with my clients. I needed to empathize with my clients through a resonance with my own woundedness, and through that empathy to read them, and access them with whatever I had to offer.

I was also becoming aware of how my clients' and my own worldviews, philosophy and spirituality affected our therapeutic process—how we define problems, set our goals and choose the means to reach them. So much of the goals and ideals of the therapeutic world have had to do with repair and resolution of our brokenness, and yet we struggle all our lives with an awareness at some level of our human limitations, flaws and vulnerabilities. They can discourage and shame us, but can also be approached from a disposition to think of our woundedness as an opportunity and challenge to stretch ourselves and dig deeper within ourselves and in our relationships to go beyond what we thought were our limitations to change and grow. To do so presumes we accept the vulnerability of our humanity and the reality that the challenge to engage it is a life-long undertaking that we cannot manage all alone. This particular journey of engagement for growth can also serve as the cornerstone of our personal differentiation because it defines our personal ideals and the path we have taken to reach them. My viewpoint about the challenges my own woundedness and vulnerabilities present me obviously colors my approach to therapy and training therapists. This perspective is the cornerstone of the philosophical and spiritual foundation of my work in therapy.

> For what matters above all is the attitude we take toward suffering, the attitude in which we take our suffering upon ourselves.
>
> (Frankl, 1963, p. 178)

> When we become aware that we do not have to escape our pains, but that we can mobilize them into a common search for life, those very pains are transformed from expressions of despair into signs of hope.
>
> (Nouwen, 1979, p. 93)

Karni Kissil

I got introduced to the POTT model in my Ph.D studies in Drexel University. I took a supervision class with Harry. As part of the class each of the students had to present a case and get supervision from Harry. I was dreading this assignment, knowing that I would have to be vulnerable in front of my classmates and discuss my "issues" and how they contribute to my difficulty with my client. I started my presentation telling myself to hang on and that in 30 minutes this difficult ordeal would be behind me, and then something happened. The way that Harry responded to my story made me forget that my classmates were in the room. My usual guardedness and defensiveness dissipated and I found myself wanting to tell him more about myself, something that rarely happened to me before. I didn't feel the need to pretend I was put together and in control. He didn't only understand me, but my feelings and behaviors made sense to him. He made me feel like a good therapist, not because I did everything right, but because I was able to acknowledge what I brought into the situation. I felt that it was "normal" to bring myself into the relationship with my clients and that bringing myself can actually help me connect with my clients. This experience was in sharp contrast to my psychodynamic training and was transformative for me. I wanted to know what exactly Harry did and how I can do that too. I wanted to help my clients feel understood and accepted like I felt.

To my amazing luck, one of the POTT trainers who taught the master's class at Drexel left and I was able to get the position. I worked with Harry and trained several generations of master's students. Together with Alba Niño (who contributed to this book), we worked to refine the model and its application in the Drexel program. We were amazed at the results we saw in our students. At the end of nine months of training their level of clinical acumen, their ability to connect with clients and above all their openness about their own vulnerability were impressive. I watched myself working with students in the same way Harry worked with me. Furthermore, I watched new generations of therapists working with their clients using what they learned in the POTT training. I had no doubts that POTT works.

We wanted to tell the world about our wonderful program and we realized that in order to do that we would have to systematically study our work. In the last few years we have conducted several studies to evaluate the effectiveness of our program and have published our findings (see 2014 article in Appendix A on p. 123, and 2013 article on p. 124). Having scientific support to the effectiveness of POTT, it is time now to disseminate the training so others can benefit. This is how I got to collaborate with Harry on this book.

Our Thinking

The relationship between client and therapist is the medium through which we gain the trust of clients, come to understand them and influence their efforts to meet their personal life challenges. This relationship is at its core personal and intimate as the therapist reaches for the innermost forces that drive peoples' lives—within themselves and in their most important personal relationships. But, it is not just the inner life of clients that is at play in this therapeutic process, but also the life of the therapist that is an active ingredient in the interactions between therapist and client. The very nature of the professional task of therapy calls for therapists to implement their learning and skills through how they use themselves with all of who they are, with all their life experience to personally connect with their clients. The effective therapist marries the professional with the personal in blends that are specific to the particular client/patient (individual, couple or family) and to the client's issue.

The training of therapists heavily invests in teaching about the development and functioning of people, offering models of thinking and intervening to effect positive change in people and solutions to their problems. However, from the very beginning of the talking therapy (think here Sigmund Freud) there has been attention on the human being who personally engages the client to utilize all of this professional learning. There has been an awareness that, however proficient we may be in our craft, we as therapists have our own personal issues that color our thinking and shape our behavior with clients, potentially to the detriment of our clients or patients. From the days of individually oriented psychoanalytic thinking to more recent systemic perspectives, trainers in the field have introduced methods of helping therapists curtail the potential toxicity of their personal hangups on their therapeutic work, geared toward resolving these personal issues through personal therapy or family interventions. More recently there has been an effort to have therapists learn to make positive use of their personal difficulties in learning to empathize with and relate to the challenges their clients face.

This is where the Person-of-the-Therapist (POTT) model of training comes in. This approach to training therapists in the use of their personal selves in the therapeutic process places special importance on working through the personal emotional "woundedness" of the therapist, which we call the therapist's "signature theme." The basic premise is that we all have certain core issues, often revolving around a main theme that has been and will be with us throughout life. This "signature theme," while from one view constitutes a stumbling block in life, from another view offers a challenge that amounts to an opportunity to stretch and transform ourselves in a myriad of ways into wiser, stronger, more caring people. Although this challenge is not likely to achieve perfect resolution, its difficulty and pain are prods to dig deeper and harder to change and improve. This life-long process reflects for therapists in its own way what therapy for our clients represents, an undertaking that involves identifying problems and working to resolve them in some form or degree to better our lives and relationships. This implies that knowing, being in touch with and engaging our personal issues can help us to better understand, relate to and address the challenges our clients face.

Our Book

After modifying and refining the POTT model and working with it for several years in various settings we felt ready to take on an incredible challenge: translating the POTT philosophy and training into a structured and detailed training manual for therapists. In this book we are charting a new path by manualizing an essential part of the training of every clinician and mental health provider: the work on the therapist's self. We take a process that seems vague and elusive, and provide a step-by-step description of how we conceptualize, operationalize and implement a training program designed to facilitate the creation of effective therapists who are skilled at using their whole selves in their encounters with their clients. This book follows the training program which we have developed and implemented in Drexel University's Couple and Family Therapy Department for more than ten years. It describes a methodology for preparing aspiring therapists to recognize and accept as normal the reality of their own flawed humanity, and then to see it and learn to use it to relate, understand and intervene more effectively with their clients. We believe that what we have garnered from our experience with this model in this setting can be adopted in other academic and non-academic contexts. In this book we present the theory and thinking behind this methodology as clearly as possible, and then demonstrate its application in as practical and vivid a way as we could to facilitate others' borrowing from it and improving on it within their own settings.

Broadly speaking, this book is designed for two groups of readers. The first group includes clinicians and supervisors who are interested in learning more about POTT. This book provides an introduction to and overview of the POTT model. We believe that clinicians and supervisors reading it will find sufficient detail to make an informed decision about whether or not POTT fits their professional needs. The information provided in this manual can provide you with a good starting point to incorporating POTT as a clinician and/or supervisor.

The second group includes program administrators and other decision-makers involved in curriculum building and implementation in clinically based mental health programs. For you, this book represents a platform upon which you can develop the competence of your trainees. As we describe in this book, the POTT model has been implemented in a variety of settings and we can work with you to modify it to add to the training resources of your facility.

The nine chapters of the book address all the various aspects of the training model. Chapter 1, *The Person-of-the-Therapist Model on the Use of Self in Therapy: The Training Philosophy*, introduces the reader to the POTT philosophy. The general perspective of the book is that therapists conduct the professional work of therapy through all of who they are personally within a very human relationship with clients that takes into account everything from culture to spirituality to family life experience to psychological challenges. We then spotlight the central and distinctive pillar of the model based on two premises: one, that we all carry within us a psychological issue that is at the core of our human woundedness, coloring our emotional functioning throughout our lives; and two, that for therapists to be able to relate most effectively to their clients, they must learn to work with and through all of who they are, but in particular through this core issue, that we call the therapist's "signature theme." The POTT model takes a unique stance regarding the value of these core psychological issues by not just suggesting that these "signature themes" are resources that can enhance therapists' effectiveness, but by placing learning to work through these signature themes at the very heart of the basic training of therapists in the use of self. In this chapter we also describe the core principles and goals of the POTT training. We describe the three components of the clinical implementation of the use of self: knowledge of self, access to self and management of self and how better mastery of self can help therapists connect, assess and intervene more effectively with their clients.

Chapter 2, *The POTT Program: Step-by-Step*, describes in detail the structure and implementation of POTT training, using an academic setting as an example—the graduate degree program in Marriage and Family Therapy at Drexel University. It includes the stages of the training, the instruments we use and case examples demonstrating each step of the training. We use vignettes to demonstrate and clarify the steps trainees take in the program from identifying their signature themes, to learning to recognize what they bring of their personal selves to their clinical encounters and to the application of what they have learned about themselves in supervised clinical experiences with families made up of trained actors.

Chapter 3, *Journaling in POTT*, highlights one component of the POTT model that offers the trainees an opportunity to reflect on an ongoing basis on how the training impacts them personally and professionally. We describe how we use journaling throughout the training to challenge, support and facilitate trainees' incorporation of the model into their clinical work. Using excerpts from journals, we also describe typical themes and processes trainees go through during the training.

Chapters 4 and 5, *The Case of Lynae* and *The Case of the "Rescuer,"* provide detailed case examples, each following one trainee throughout her entire journey in a nine-month POTT training course. The trainees' written assignments and transcripts of their signature theme presentations are used to demonstrate how we work with trainees and the process they go through in the program, and to highlight from their perspectives the effects on them of different aspects of the POTT training.

Chapter 6, *About the Facilitators*, covers the implementation of the POTT model focusing on the facilitators. We describe how the facilitators are trained, the basic requirements and qualifications of the facilitators and what exactly the facilitators do throughout the training to make the POTT model effective and safe for the trainees.

Chapter 7, *Integrating POTT into Your Setting: Applications and Modifications*, describes possible adaptations of POTT to various settings and facilities. It answers questions such as "how to use POTT without a simulation lab?" "can POTT be modified to be used in supervision?" and "how POTT can be adapted to non-academic settings such as mental health centers and private practices?" This chapter also includes some of the nuts and bolts involved in implementing POTT, such as structural and time requirements, and the training of actors to perform as client families.

Chapter 8, *POTT Principles across Mental Health Disciplines: "Just Use Your Clinical Judgment,"* demonstrates how the POTT principles are relevant and applicable across mental health disciplines (e.g. marriage and family therapy, counseling, psychology and social work). This chapter's specific discussion points include understanding the development of clinical judgment through the POTT philosophy as related to the practice-related educational standards of various professional and accrediting organizations. In order to fully equip trainees to engage with diverse clients, educators require a solid framework for helping them build their clinical judgment. POTT serves as a developmental platform for preparing trainees to use themselves effectively while building therapeutic relationships, assessing clients and creating intentional interventions. The chapter offers a very personal narrative of how all this is played out in one trainee's training experience.

The ninth and last chapter in the book, *Supervision in the POTT Model*, provides an in depth description of the adaptation of the POTT model to clinical supervision as differentiated from training, using a detailed case example.

This book is the result of a joint effort by several POTT model enthusiasts. Thus, we cannot end the Preface without thanking our co-authors who have made significant contributions to this book: Renata Carneiro, Christian Jordal, Alba Niño, Jody Russon and Senem Zeytinoglu. All of us have been involved in the POTT training at Drexel University, either as instructors or teaching assistants, and we all took part in refining the model and making the training more effective each year. We all share the vision of facilitating the development of effective clinicians by introducing the POTT training model to other programs, supervisors and clinicians. Thank you for your hard work and for sharing our vision!

Harry J. Aponte and Karni Kissil

References

Frankl, V.E. (1963). *Man's search for meaning.* New York: Washington Square Press.
Nouwen, H.J.M. (1979). *The wounded healer.* New York: Image.

Acknowledgments

We want to acknowledge our debt to Dr. Marlene Watson, who when head of Drexel's Couple and Family Therapy program had the confidence in the POTT model to have been instrumental in incorporating it into the core training of the students, and then to have prodded us year after year to publish on the model. We also want to thank Dr. Stephanie Brooks for continuing to wholeheartedly encourage the development of the model within the Couple and Family Therapy Department. This book would not have come into existence without your help and support. Finally, we would like to express our gratitude to our trainees and supervisees. Your courage and trust have helped us in the development of the POTT model and the refinement of the training. Your contribution to this book is invaluable.

Harry J. Aponte and Karni Kissil

1 The Person-of-the-Therapist Model on the Use of Self in Therapy

The Training Philosophy

Harry J. Aponte

The Training Philosophy of the POTT Approach

The main thrust of the POTT model has to do with a use of self that emanates from the personal depths of the individual who is conducting the therapy. This is more than a strategy about how therapists use themselves. This is about us, as clinicians, developing a conscious, purposeful and disciplined access to our humanity within our professional role in the therapeutic relationship. This means that as therapists we view the therapeutic process, at its core, as a person-to-person human encounter. The POTT approach assumes that the more both therapist and client are experientially present in this living process of therapy, the greater the access the therapist has to self and to client to do the work of therapy. POTT's concept of being "present" in the therapeutic relationship implies a professionally tailored purposeful *personal* engagement with the client (individual, couple or family) that lends clarity of insight, depth of sensitivity and potency of effectiveness to the therapist's clinical performance.

That encounter in session is a *living experience* among family members and between therapist and client. Whatever the therapeutic model, when therapist and client (family, couple or individual) come together in a session, they engage in the common task of therapy, which generates a human system with its own unique to the moment complex of dynamics. Even as the narrative therapist consciously focuses on constructing or deconstructing a story with a family (West & Bubenzer, 2000) there is personal engagement between them that affects all parties involved and their relationships with each other, and therefore the course of the therapy. A structural family therapist can witness or actively coax interactions among the clients themselves when it is a couple or a family. In the enactment, a human connection is activated among the parties that connects minds and hearts in deeply personal ways that give a unique color and shape to the therapeutic process. Classical psychoanalysts foster those human connections in their silence, which triggers transference that incites countertransference, again affecting all parties in profoundly human ways (Bochner, 2000). The psychoanalyst may perceive through the inner experience of the "Third Ear," by hearing "the voices [of the patient] from within the self that are otherwise not audible" (Reik, 1948, p. 147). These personal transactional effects in all therapeutic methods become integral to the therapeutic process. Whether we are attending primarily to technique based on the articulation of language, the drama of human interaction or the perception of the projection of an unconscious introject, these are transactional processes within the therapeutic relationship that facilitate the understanding and promote the therapeutic change of therapy.

We take the position that the relationship in therapy, whether recognized or not by the therapeutic model, is a critical factor through which all therapies achieve positive change. Note Weiss and colleagues (2015):

> Most of the research on the therapeutic alliance has been conducted with therapies that emphasize the relationship as an essential mechanism of (e.g., psychodynamic or humanistic orientations), but results appear to be similar for treatments that do not emphasize the relationship as the main mechanism of change.
>
> (p. 29)

See Muntigl and Horvath (2015):

> Over the last three decades empirical research has provided robust support for the general claim that the quality of the therapeutic relationship bears a ubiquitous and significant relation to treatment outcome across the breadth of client problems and variety of treatment approaches.
>
> (p. 41)

These claims lead to two critical questions: How does the therapeutic relationship make therapy work? How do we train therapists to use the therapeutic relationship to achieve their goals? These questions are particularly intriguing since we are looking at this relational process between therapist and client in the contexts of the full range of therapeutic modalities and therapeutic components.

The POTT perspective asserts both that we as therapists are active agents in the dynamic, living experience of the therapeutic relationship to relate, assess and intervene with clients, and that our level of expertise can be enhanced through training. Therapists can decide the degree and manner in which they wish to be present and work through the forces of their personal connections and interactions with clients. For example, when talking about the technique of "enactment" in which family members are prompted to interact around their issues, family therapists "can engage in a facilitating manner from inside the family transaction by participating in it, or from outside by not engaging directly in the transaction" (Aponte & VanDeusen, 1981, p. 325). Structural therapists do this as an integral part of their model (Minuchin & Fishman, 1981). Dattilio includes a form of enactment in his cognitive-behavioral approach to working with families (2010). In talking about attachment-based therapies, Wylie and Turner (2011) state that, "much or even most of this therapy is intuitive, played out in 'enactments'" (p. 27). "The core emotionally focused therapy intervention is *restructuring interactions*" (p. 117), which Sprenkle and colleagues (2009) assert is worked through the enactment. Whether or not the enactment or any other technique is explicitly scripted in our approach, we as therapists choose consciously or unconsciously what to do with ourselves personally vis-à-vis our clients when intervening with them. As such, we can be emotionally present or absent, open or closed, connected or disengaged, active or passive, etc. However, as therapists, for that connection with the client to be *purposeful*, it must be conscious on our part, and for it to be *professionally* purposeful, it must be actively directed by us toward articulated therapeutic ends.

The POTT approach views the personal connection in the therapeutic relationship as a factor common to all therapies in the sense that in all approaches we face the challenge, consciously or subliminally, to assume a genuine personal relational posture with respect to clients that fits our own and our clients' personalities and backgrounds, the issue of the moment, and our therapeutic ideologies. Because of the POTT perspective about the impact of the personal component on the therapeutic relationship, the model emphasizes the importance of us as therapists being able to both identify with and differentiate ourselves from our clients. We should be able to engage the client most aptly clinically while maintaining in that clinically decisive moment the most therapeutically effective professional distance. With respect to the relationship, ultimately the goal is for us to connect closely enough to gain that moment's clinically necessary accessibility to the client while remaining free in the relationship to perform the requisite professional task.

Identification and Differentiation

For a therapist to be able at any given moment to integrate these polar opposites (personal and professional) within the role of therapist, we will need to be able to both personally identify with and differentiate from our client(s) as required clinically at any particular moment in the therapeutic process. This identification calls for our being able to see ourselves in the client's issue at the appropriate moment, in some way getting in touch with the facet of the client's struggle with which we need to then resonate through an awareness and connection with some relevant trace of our own human frailty and vulnerability. This empathic resonance has both affective and cognitive elements (Gerdes & Segal, 2011). As therapists we need to be able to both feel with our clients, and be conscious of the nature of the connection. The resonance can be with the client's issue that may in some part of the *issue* have even a trace resemblance to a personal issue of ours. The resonance can also or even only find a reflection in how the client and we *struggle* with our respective issues that in themselves can be quite different. We look to feel what it is like to walk in the client's shoes just enough to realize a personal sense of the client's experience as needed to carry out a therapeutic task.

However, to be able to achieve this intimate connection in the moment and still operate with the emotional independence of a professional, we must also be able to differentiate from the client and the client's experience, much along Bowen's concept of differentiation, which speaks to a relative personal autonomy and freedom from emotional fusion with others (Bowen, 1972; Kerr, 1981), but from the POTT perspective relative to what is needed in the moment of the therapeutic process. In the general perspective, differentiation, as POTT uses the term, has to do with our sense of self and grounding in self. It touches on our emotional responsiveness as ensconced in the strength of our personal boundaries that are shaped by commitment to our personal ideals and the journey to the personal goals connoted by those ideals. At the level of our functioning in the role of therapist in the clinical moment, this concept of differentiation speaks to the ability to be connected to the point of identification with a client, while also retaining the freedom to relate, assess and intervene with clients as stipulated by the therapeutic needs of our client in the now.

Pursuing these ends requires that therapists work toward:

1. *Knowledge of Self:* Therapists look to understand themselves in the moment by continually studying and examining how their past and their present impinge on who they are today. Self-insight includes the psychological and relational aspects of our lives, along with the personal worldviews, values, morality and social location that color not only our vision of our clients and our clients' issues, but also our own philosophies about change in therapy.
2. *Access to Self:* As they engage with clients, therapists reach to access their memories, emotions, spirituality and social consciousness relevant *at the moment* to the therapeutic process. This is much more than intellectually recalling them. It means being in touch with what belongs to self, and is inside of self so as to draw from within ourselves into the living moment of the therapeutic encounter whatever aspects of our life experience, personal makeup and philosophical/spiritual perspectives are needed for the therapeutic tasks of forming relationships, assessing and intervening in the clinical instance.
3. *Management of Self:* For therapists to purposefully use whatever they need of themselves when called for, we need the *discernment* and *discipline* to selectively open ourselves to the client and the client's issues, and to activate and project the specific aspects of ourselves that are needed for the therapeutic task of the moment.

Self-insight, self-access and self-management cannot be simply willed. For all of us there are things about ourselves that we do not want to face. Doing so will hurt, make us anxious or discouraged, or cause us shame. There are aspects of our inner or relational lives that we avoid being in touch with because we cannot tolerate what we feel when we touch the memories or emotions attached to them. And there are parts of ourselves over which we have little control to our embarrassment or dismay. Yet, these discomforting facets of ourselves are treasures of human experience that bond us to the rest of humanity and can allow us to resonate empathically with our brothers and sisters. There are also parts of ourselves that we so take for granted that we are unaware of the extent to which they shade and shape how we see and relate to people and their lives. These may be attitudes and values that are part of our family legacies, culture or spirituality. Unless we are conscious of them we cannot make active use of them therapeutically, cannot take them into account when we interpret and evaluate what we see and hear of our clients.

As therapists, we need to be able to work with all of who we are within the various component tasks of the therapeutic process at the appropriate clinical moment. Yet, we will need help, and we argue here—training that specifically enables us to see, reach and actively utilize all these parts of ourselves as needed, when needed. It also happens that any training process that succeeds in gaining us such personal insight, access and governance of ourselves within our roles as therapists will likely also spark personal change in us. Any such change in us in the POTT model is not directly intended, although it is welcomed, especially if it helps us to do better therapy, which is what POTT is all about. To the question of whether that makes the POTT training therapy, the answer is "no" because those personal changes are not the essential or primary goals of the training. The basic aim of the POTT training model is to give the therapist greater freedom and skill in the use of the self to conduct better therapy. The trainers assume responsibility for helping to produce better therapists, not to help people resolve their personal issues although if in the process of the training they happen to contribute to people's efforts to improve themselves personally, the trainers will be happy they did. We will examine here what it means to work on self to enhance our therapeutic skills.

Let us consider some very brief examples of how therapists may utilize their personal selves to carry out some therapeutic tasks. We must have the self-insight, be able to access the called-for place within ourselves, and then put into an actionable place that part-of-self required by the task at hand. We may even need to draw from within ourselves a mental and emotional disposition that may not come easily to us to carry out a therapeutic task in a particular situation with a particular client. For example, in one actual instance, a therapist's goal was to gain the trust of an especially well-defended client. For the therapist, remaining open and engaged in the face of the woman's emotional lockdown was a difficult challenge because of a core emotional issue of his own, the drive to attain his goals, in this case a palpable therapeutic outcome, which he experienced her as blocking.

The client hides her insecurities and vulnerability behind her considerable ability to intellectualize, discouraging the therapist's inquisitiveness. The therapist feels the wall of self-protection. Knowing himself, he resists his natural impulse to push against it, and consciously (self-management) puts himself in the mindset of just wondering, "Why the wall?" He looks within himself (self-access) for the barriers he knows well (self-knowledge) that he puts up to protect his own vulnerabilities. In this self-reflection about his personal manner of going it alone, he finds the bridge to identify and empathize with his client's need to protect her self. He can then access within himself at the appropriate moment an empathically felt desire to engage her in talking about the wall, enabling him to substitute interest and caring for the familiar urge of his to uncover for the sake of an outcome. She appears to experience the therapist as sensitive to her need to protect herself. She responds as if it is safe enough to trust his query, and allow a degree of emotional vulnerability for the beginning at that moment of a real connection in the journey of their therapeutic relationship.

In another example of use of self- knowledge, self-access and self-management, a therapist resonates with a couple to better assess and intervene. Speaking about attunement in attachment-based therapy, Wylie and Turner (2011) describe this connection as "the therapist's whole self vibrated like a tuning fork to every quiver in the client's being" (p. 25). In this case, a therapist hypothesizes that their respective fears of being let down by the other are tearing the couple's relationship apart. The therapist strategically chooses to work through identification with the man, who appears to be feeling most emotionally vulnerable at that moment.

The husband cuts himself off emotionally from his wife when he feels challenged by her need for emotional intimacy. The therapist encourages the two to engage with each other about their issue right then. He opens himself up (self-access) to experience what he sees in the husband, and soon begins to resonate with the man's insecurity about being able to be present to his wife as emotionally open and giving of himself as she needs. The therapist allows himself to connect to his own parallel insecurities, and feels something of what the man feels. The therapist talks to the man from that source of insecurity within himself (self-management) what similar feelings he intuits the man struggles with. The man seems to feel understood, and begins to let up on his guard. With the therapist's support and coaching, the man tells his wife right there that his withdrawal at such a time is not because he does not care about her, but because of his fear that he will fail her, that what he has to offer of himself will not be enough. His words offer her some reassurance about his love, allowing her to begin to let go of her own fear of rejection, and tentatively open up to him right then in the session.

These illustrations offer a glimpse of what therapists commonly do, but often without full consciousness of what they reached for within themselves to make that empathic connection. But, these cases also provide examples of how therapists can *consciously* and *deliberately* manage their own emotional state and cognitive outlook to predispose themselves personally to what they are attempting in a professional role. The underlying assumptions about what is basically required for the effective use of self are common factors in virtually all therapies that work through the relationship between therapist and client. The broad therapeutic objectives for the use of self that are at least implicitly shared with other therapeutic approaches and that can be considered common factors in this regard are:

1. **The Relationship**: The therapist, present to the *now* moment, uses self *actively* and *purposefully* to connect personally with the client in the therapeutic manner this therapy calls for with this client at this time.

2. **The Assessment**: The therapist reaches within self by *personal ac* the empathic key to the client's experience that best prepares the th to *understand* the client and the client's issue in the clinical moment.

3. **The Intervention**: The therapist tailors a *personal disposition* toward the client within a specifically selected therapeutic posture to implement the technical *intervention* now intended.

The Relationship: *The therapist uses self actively and purposefully to achieve the connection that this therapy with this client calls for at this time.*

Therapists assume relational postures vis-à-vis their clients as part of the conceptual structure of their therapeutic viewpoints. Giving life to those relational structures are personal human relationships that lend a particular quality to the therapeutic relational framework.

While some models do not, others have very clear concepts about the relational posture therapists should assume vis-à-vis clients to operate according to the tenets of the model. The professional posture dictated by the school of therapy presents a corresponding personal challenge for the therapist. For example, postmodern approaches to therapy advocate a democratic, i.e. a collaborative relationship between therapist and client where power is shared co-equally. Harlene Anderson (1997), for instance, describes the meeting of therapist and client in a postmodern approach: "They [clients] became engaged with us in a partnered process of coexploring the problem and codeveloping the possibilities" (p. 63). The goal is parity between client and therapist in the relational process. From the POTT perspective, the personal challenge for the therapist in this postmodern context is to cede a degree of personal control, consciously allowing a degree of vulnerability that facilitates a genuine personal mutuality between therapist and client appropriate to the clinical task of the moment.

At the other end of the spectrum from their perspective on structural family therapy, Minuchin and Fishman (1981) describe the role of the therapist and consequently the nature of the therapist–client relationship in these terms: "When the therapist and the family members join a therapeutic system, they enter into an explicit contract that defines the therapist as the expert of the system and the leader of the therapeutic endeavor" (p. 161). The power scale tilts toward the therapist. The personal challenge for the therapist in this context is to take ownership of the responsibility to direct and guide the therapeutic process without robbing the clients of their personal freedom within the transaction, but in a manner that fits the needs of that moment.

Carl Rogers (Baldwin, 2013) speaks of the role of the therapist vis-à-vis the client as being "very clearly, obviously present" (p. 28). However, he goes on to place the power in the therapeutic relationship not between therapist and client or in the therapist's hands, but in the hands of the client. As he puts it: "I became convinced that the final authority lies with the individual and that there is no real external authority that can be depended upon" (p. 32).

Here, the personal challenge for the therapist is to open the therapeutic process to the client's power and freedom to choose while still intimately be engaged and present to the client, again aligned with the clinical intention of that instant.

For one therapist, any of these relational postures vis-à-vis his/her client may come easily and naturally in a particular situation, while for another it may require digging deeply into self to find a way that synchronizes the therapist's natural human disposition with the strategic stance that the therapeutic model calls for now.

The POTT model speaks to certain common elements in the therapeutic relationship, and breaks these down under the headings of identifying with clients and differentiating from clients. Under *identification* some of these core elements of the therapeutic relationship involve therapists looking to:

- Discover within our selves issues and their underlying dynamics that in some way resonate with those of our clients in any particular circumstance.
- Find as needed similarities and/or parallels in our own lives to the clients' socioeconomic backgrounds, ethnicities, cultural fabrics and personal values, especially those that pertain to the issues that are the focus of the therapy.
- Dispose our selves emotionally to want to care about and connect personally with our clients by searching in their histories and struggles for points of resonance relevant to our therapeutic goals of the moment or stage of therapy.

Under *differentiation* some of these common elements involve our looking to:

- Identify where we end and our clients begin in their interactions within the therapeutic process, particularly where our *professional responsibility* to help ends and where the clients' freedom to choose to change begins at any point in the therapeutic process.
- Recognize the moment where our *personal connections* with our clients meet and end at the boundaries of the professional frameworks of our codes and models within which we are working with the clients.
- Attend, as we especially need to remain differentiated at any stage of the process, to the observational, analytic and strategic processes of our professional roles that transcend the personal dynamics operating within the relational process.

In the POTT model we train to utilize our personal selves to potentiate our professional activities within the therapeutic process, in the instance of the existential experience of the therapeutic relationship. Specifically with regard to the relationship, the POTT goals for us are to foster empathy toward, acceptance of and connection with our client particularly around the client's woundedness that resonates with our own personal woundedness in relation to the demands of the therapeutic situation.

The Assessment: *The therapist reaches within him/her self to discover the empathic key to a personal connection with the client that best prepares the therapist to read and assess the client and the client's issues appropriate to the demands of the therapeutic process.*

Virtually all therapists recognize that they come to know their clients through the medium of their relationship with the client. We speak here of a "personal knowing," the raw data of people's personal experience of life from which we draw the data that forms the basis of our speculations and hypotheses about diagnoses and formulations about patterns of thinking, behaving and relating.

The affinity of an engagement at a personal level makes possible a relationship where clients know they are known by us in ways that others do not know them. In the context of that therapeutic encounter, which Satir (2000) describes as the "intimate experience" (p. 22), therapists make professional observations, sensing and feeling their clients' pain and struggles, as well as their strengths. To this end, we must be able to *resonate* at a human level with our clients; from an attachment-based therapy lexicon, have the "capacity for emotional attunement" (Wylie & Turner, 2011, p. 23) as required in any clinical instance.

More specifically in relation to that intimate experience, we identify with our clients in order to understand them, whether or not we are fully aware of it. We "get" what is humanly going on with clients because we share that same humanity. We can consciously train ourselves to search within ourselves reflexively for some feeling, personal conviction or life experience that resonates with whatever the client is experiencing in session. On the other hand, at any moment we can emotionally and cognitively open ourselves up to a client's take on and emotional reaction to a personal experience of theirs that is alien to us. Such an experience for us may flip on the light of a new insight into what is ailing the client. Both identification and differentiation can illuminate the client for a therapist.

We have already spoken about the therapist's openness and vulnerability in the relationship with the client. This personal openness to the client not only sets the stage for the relationship that is the foundation upon which the therapy builds, it is also the disposition of the therapist that allows us to sense and perceive the client at deeper levels that may include the subconscious. The vulnerability involved in this openness permits us as therapists to reverberate and resonate to what clients communicate through their words and actions, and their very presence in our space. This openness, which we can regulate as the clinical situation calls for, is the empathic key to grasping their message, feeling their emotions and getting where they come from. Vulnerability in this sense means that our person can serve as a mirror into which we can receive another's image with its emotional and spiritual shadings, and through which we can see and understand that individual or family with whom we engage beyond what our senses consciously see and hear of them. Together with our sensory detectors, this inner reading enables us to perceive and decipher at both cognitive and intuitive levels.

Finally, for therapists to resonate that closely with our clients, we must also have enough distance from the client that we can "see" the client. Kerr (1981) speaks of the therapist's differentiation from the Bowenian perspective:

> People towards the upper end of the scale [of differentiation] are people in whom the individuality and togetherness forces approach an optimum mix or balance, a balance that permits the person to be a well-defined individual in his/her own right as well as an effective team player.
>
> (pp. 246–247)

All therapists recognize the need to maintain a certain professional distance so as to form judgments about what they observe of their clients. From the POTT perspective, therapists need to be grounded in their own personal journeys and spirituality, even as they are grounded in their professional cognition and skills (Aponte, 1998). For POTT this is a dynamic concept— an authentic personal presence and connection vis-à-vis the client, coexisting with an observing professional stance that allows for the freedom of professional judgment and action fitted and adapted to the needs of the therapeutic situation.

Under identification and differentiation some of these core elements of the assessment process in the therapy involve us first with regard to identification looking to:

- Open our selves mentally and emotionally, resonant to the clinical instance, to observe the flow and manifestations of our clients' thinking, feelings and pain.
- Open our selves to ourselves to perceive and identify our own reactions and associations to what we are experiencing in the moment within the relationship with the clients.

With regard to differentiation we are looking to take distance by:

- Tracking within our selves the connections between what our clients are overly communicating and what we directly experience of our clients within our selves.
- Monitoring continuously the degree of synchrony between the data we are gathering directly and interiorly and our clinical hypotheses and therapeutic strategies.

With regard to the assessment process the POTT goals for us are to foster a personal sensitivity toward what the client communicates to the point that we can intuit in the *now* moment what is happening with the client through our own associations to and personal experience of the client.

The Intervention: *The therapist tailors, as needed in the moment, a personal disposition toward the client within a specifically selected therapeutic posture to implement the technical intervention.*

"To induce change, every systemic model focuses on altering the affect, behavior, and/or cognitions of at least one participant in an interactional cycle" (Sprenkle et al., 2009, p. 110). At a personal level, we must have the command of self as needed in the moment to dispose ourselves mentally and emotionally in a way that enables the execution of an intervention that reaches the participant(s) in that cycle as it is meant to touch and be received by the client(s).

We all consciously or unconsciously choose a relational posture for the implementation of a therapeutic strategy or technical intervention. In some therapeutic approaches these personal postures vis-à-vis clients are made explicit. At one extreme, classical psychoanalysts relate to patients in ways that encourage reflection and regression by remaining relatively anonymous as called for at stages of the therapeutic process to encourage transference, which is represented physically by placing the therapist's chair behind and out of sight of the client who is lying on a couch. In stark contrast, Minuchin and Fishman (1981) propose an example of their approach when they intend to "unbalance" the structure of a family: "The therapist will have to use herself, as a member of the therapeutic system, to challenge and change the family power allocation" (p. 161). In another contrast, Jeffrey Koob (2009), speaking of solution-focused brief therapy offers the example of when "an SFBT therapist takes the stance of being nonconfrontational" (p. 158) as he/she alters "the focus from problem talk to solution talk (i.e., the positives in their lives)" (p. 151). Whether we are attempting to remain relatively anonymous, actively challenge a client or avoid confrontation for a positive approach, at a personal level we will need to be able at the appropriate time and manner to personally dispose our attitudes, thinking and feelings to fit our interventional goals.

Under identification some of these core elements of the interventional process in the therapy involve us first looking to:

- Infuse our interventions at will with our personal emotional and cognitive dispositions that synch with what the clients themselves are then disposed to take in.
- Ensconce in the appropriate circumstances our interventions within the socio-cultural framework of our clients through the associations we have made through our own socio-cultural experiences.
- Maneuver adroitly in our relationships with our clients so as to work through the openness our clients' trust affords us at any given moment.

With regard to differentiation therapists are looking to:

- Intervene from a place of personal freedom that fits where we need to be in the relationships with our clients because of our comfort and flexibility within our own personal journeys.

- Intervene as needed from the clarity about and commitment to our own professional roles within the complex and multilayered relationships we have with our clients.

With regard to the interventional process, the POTT goal for us as therapists is to foster a personally sensitive disposition that is best suited to where the client is in the relationship with us and what the client needs therapeutically at the moment of contact.

From the POTT perspective, none of the above should be assumed. Training and supervision can target the development of the capacity for complexity and range of personal connections to clients, and the discipline required to personally dispose our selves in our professional roles as needed within the therapeutic relationship with our clients.

Conclusion

The POTT perspective posits that the personal use of self can be trained, refined and enhanced to make for more effective therapy. Through enhanced insight into our selves, conscious and deliberate access to that self, and trained skill in the use of that self, therapists can relate, assess and intervene actively and purposefully within the framework of their therapeutic models, whatever they may be. This training and supervision can rest on common factors recognized as foundational to any sound therapeutic approach. It can reflect closely a particular therapeutic model or a systematic integration of approaches that appeals to the individual therapist. The common thread is how we, as therapists, consciously and purposefully work through our humanity to relate, assess and intervene therapeutically.

References

Anderson, H. (1997). *Conversation, language, and possibilities: A postmodern approach to therapy.* New York: Basic Books.

Aponte, H.J. (1998). Intimacy in the therapist-client relationship. In W.J. Matthews & J.H. Edgette (Eds.), *Current thinking and research in brief therapy: Solutions, strategies, narratives. (Vol. II)* (pp. 3–27). Philadelphia: Taylor & Francis.

Aponte, H.J. & VanDeusen, J.M. (1981). Structural family therapy. In A.S. Gurman & D.P. Kniskern (Eds.), *Handbook of family therapy* (pp. 310–360). New York: Brunner/Mazel.

Baldwin, M. (2013). Interview with Carl Rogers on the use of the self in therapy. In M. Baldwin (Ed.), *The use of self in therapy* (3rd ed., pp. 28–35). New York: Routledge.

Bochner, D.A. (2000). *The therapist's use of self in family therapy.* Northvale, NJ: Jason Aronson.

Bowen, M. (1972). Toward a differentiation of a self in one's family. In James L. Framo (Ed.), *Family interaction* (pp. 111–173). New York: Springer.

Dattilio, F.M. (2010). *Cognitive-behavior therapy with couples and families: A comprehensive guide for clinicians*. New York: Guilford.

Gerdes, K.E. & Segal, E.A. (2011). The importance of empathy for social work practice: Integrating new science. *Social Work, 56*(2), 141–148.

Kerr, M.E. (1981). Family systems theory and therapy. In A.S. Gurman, & D.P. Kniskern (Eds.), *Handbook of family therapy* (pp. 226–264). New York: Brunner/Mazel.

Koob, J.J. (2009). Solution-focused family interventions. In A.C. Kilpatrick & T.P. Holland (Eds.), *Working with families* (pp. 147–169). Boston: Allyn & Bacon.

Minuchin, S. & Fishman, H.C. (1981). *Family therapy techniques*. Cambridge, MA: Harvard University Press.

Muntigl, P. & Horvath, A.O. (2015). The therapeutic relationship in action: How therapists and clients co-manage relational disaffiliation. In H. Wiseman & O. Tishby (Eds.), *The therapeutic relationship: Innovative investigations* (pp. 41–59). London: Routledge.

Reik, T. (1948). *Listening with the third ear*. New York: Ferrar, Straus and Giroux.

Satir, V. (2000). The therapist story. In M. Baldwin (Ed.), *The use of self in therapy* (2nd ed., pp. 17–28). New York: Haworth.

Sprenkle, D.H., Davis, S.D. & Lebow, J.L. (2009). *Common factors in couple and family therapy*. New York: Guilford.

Weiss, M., Kivity, Y. & Huppert, J.D. (2015). How does the therapeutic alliance develop throughout cognitive behavioral therapy for panic disorder? Sawtooth patterns, sudden gains, and stabilization. In H. Wiseman & O. Tishby (Eds.), *The therapeutic relationship: Innovative investigations* (pp. 29–40). London: Routledge.

West, J.D. & Bubenzer, D.L. (2000). Narrative family therapy. In J. Carlson & D. Kjos (Eds.), *Theories and strategies of family therapy* (pp. 353–381). Boston: Allyn and Bacon.

Wylie, M.S. & Turner, L. (2011). The attuned therapist. *Psychotherapy Networker, 35*, 18–27, 48–49.

2 The POTT Program
Step-by-Step

Senem Zeytinoglu

The POTT model saw its beginnings in Philadelphia in the late seventies when Harry Aponte ran groups for clinicians looking to develop their skills in the use of their own persons in family therapy. The program continued its development at the Family Institute of Virginia in Richmond, where it is still running today, under the label of the Person/Practice Model (Aponte & Winter, 2013).

The director of Drexel University's Couple and Family Therapy Department, Marlene Watson, was the person who proposed the idea of establishing this training in an academic setting, specifically, the Marriage and Family Therapy master's program at Drexel University. Watson believed that the POTT model provided a foundation for a systemic training on the use of self for students of family therapy, and invited Harry Aponte to test this model for the first time in an academic setting at Drexel University (Aponte et al., 2009).

The POTT model had its first run in Drexel's Couple and Family Therapy program in 2002 as a no-credit, pilot training involving six trainees who participated as volunteers. The positive experiences of the volunteering trainees (Lutz & Irizarry, 2009) along with the faculty's perception of the clinical growth of the students who participated in the program led to the integration of the training into the curriculum. Currently, POTT is a mandatory, year-long course for all first year master's trainees (Aponte et al., 2009).

The POTT course at Drexel University runs for three of four quarters—fall, winter and spring (see Appendices A.1, B.1 and C.1 for syllabi). It is divided into two sections with an effort to limit the classes to 12 students each. Two facilitators run each section with the help of two graduate assistants. The first quarter's focus is on helping trainees identify and present on their signature themes, meaning what they consider to be the personal issues most dominant in their lives. The second quarter has the students presenting cases, preferably illustrated by video, in which they look to recognize how a client family and its issues affect them personally in a clinical encounter, and in particular how their signature themes are triggered in their process with a client family. In the third quarter, trainees conduct therapy sessions with a simulated client family or couple (called "simulated laboratory" or "simlab"). Paid actors assume the roles of members of the client family or the couple. Each student conducts a session with the client receiving live supervision from the two facilitators. This simlab experience is designed for the trainees to practice the use of their signature themes and personal life experiences to relate, assess and intervene with clients.

Even though these are the set components of the POTT course, the structure and the order of the components are flexible and subject to change based on the number of trainees. The only exception is that we always start with helping trainees identify their signature themes, and then understand how these themes manifest themselves in their clinical work, and finally provide them with an experience of applying what they learned to a client family (simulated). In this chapter we offer detailed descriptions of each presentation topic, and review the various components of the training process.

The Structure and Components of the Training

Two Introductory Classes to the POTT Philosophy and Training Program

In the first session of the training, the facilitators introduce the POTT model and describe its core philosophy and primary goals. They orient the students to the training program, explaining each step and its requirements. We start by asking the trainees to read certain publications on the POTT model, and mark the quotes that were most meaningful to them. We devote the next session to the sharing of the quotes and processing them with the group.

We ask the trainees right from the beginning to write a journal entry after every class (see Appendix A.1 for a journal writing guide, which is in the syllabus). This entry, which is usually not to be more than a page long, should include how the class affected them, in particular what came up for them about their own personal issues when other trainees present on some personal issue of theirs that may affect their clinical practice. These journals are read by the two facilitators of the class and the two graduate assistants, with the latter giving feedback to the trainees about their insights and personal reactions to what they witnessed in the fellow trainees' presentations. The graduate assistants also look to offer ongoing, personal and individualized support to the trainees both in writing and in personal meetings with them. The program recognizes that the process trainees undergo can have a profound emotional impact on them, and that faculty members need to be alert to what each trainee may need in the personally demanding process of the training. We will go into greater detail about this component of the training in the next chapter.

Personal Presentations: Identifying Your Signature Theme

The first training task of POTT is to help trainees identify their signature themes, and describe their evolution and impact on their personal and professional lives. In this process, we ask our trainees to explore their personal life struggles, coping mechanisms and patterns of functioning. The trainees are asked to write a paper about their theme and then present on it in class. Below are some questions that we ask our trainees to reflect upon prior to writing their signature theme paper. We found these questions helpful in clarifying the concept of the signature theme:

- What is your biggest source of anxiety and/or biggest fear? (e.g. being abandoned, rejected, not being good enough, failing at an important endeavor, etc.)
- Is there something about yourself that you would prefer people not to know? What do you do to keep people from knowing this?
- Is there a characteristic of yours that somehow limits you in your functioning and relationships? (e.g. not wanting to feel needy, thus pretending to be self-sufficient and not asking for the help you need, and so feeling alone.)
- How do you usually deal with stress? Do you have a reaction to stressful situations or interactions that seems to cause you problems?
- Looking back at your life, can you recognize a recurrent pattern in your functioning and/or relationships that doesn't work well for you?

We emphasize to our trainees that signature themes are not specific events or relationships, but rather personal patterns of feeling, thinking and relating shaped by those events and relationships. We also tell them that it is possible that in the beginning of this process they will identify several signature themes. However, these multiple themes usually get consolidated into one or two overarching themes through the signature theme presentations.

The trainees' first task is to submit a paper on their signature theme (see Appendix A.3 for a guide to writing the signature theme paper). The paper is submitted to both facilitators and graduate assistants a few days before their presentation. This paper consists of five sections, which are: (1) description of the therapist's signature theme, (2) the therapist's genogram, (3) the therapist's family history as related to the signature theme, (4) the current manifestation of the therapist's signature theme, and the therapist's struggle with the theme's issues, and (5) the signature theme's actual and/or potential impact on the therapist's clinical work.

Below are the specific instructions for the signature theme paper:

1. **Signature Theme**
    Describe what you believe to be the personal issue that has been most dominant in your life. This is the hangup of yours that has and continues to vex you, affecting many or all areas of your life. Take into consideration the emotional, spiritual and social components of your life when describing your issue.

2. **Genogram**
    Attach a three generational genogram of your family, with comments that may help us understand who the characters are and their relationships to one another.

3. **Family History**

    Provide a history of your family, as you believe it relates to your signature theme. These are your hypotheses about ways your family members and your relationships with them may have contributed to the origin and perpetuation of your signature theme.

4. **The Struggle with Your Signature Theme**

    Speak to how you deal with your signature theme. Here describe where you handle it poorly, and where you deal with it most effectively. Add who in your life is least helpful and most helpful to you in wrestling with it.

5. **Your Clinical Work**

    Offer your thoughts to how you believe your signature theme has affected or may affect your relationship with clients and your work with their issues—negatively and positively.

In the example below, you can read brief excerpts from a trainee's signature theme paper; she describes her signature theme, her family history, her current struggle with her signature theme and how it impacts her clinical work. Excerpts from other papers of this trainee will be presented in this chapter to serve as a guide for the reader to understand the content of each assignment. We present two complete case studies (in Chapters 4 and 5) to illustrate the whole process a trainee goes through during the training.

Identification of the Signature Theme

Neither of my parents really abandoned us; they were always a part of our lives but I still felt as though I had been abandoned and/or rejected by my father. I believe that the fear of rejection and abandonment is my signature theme. Growing up, I had this attitude that made people not want to mess with me. I never fought people or bullied people but I would speak my mind and people were scared of me.

Family History

My parents had their three other children and from the little I remember, we had good times. When I was about six, my mom found out my dad was having an affair with her best friend. They decided to divorce and he married my stepmom very quickly. The impact this had on my mom majorly affected our lives. When my mom found out about the affair, she was pregnant. My father said he didn't want any more children with her so she believed by having an abortion, it may save their marriage. It didn't . . .

Current Struggle with the Signature Theme

If I am in a situation like starting school or moving to a new place, I will be more extroverted and friendly just to meet new people. However, I am constantly worried that people will think I am stupid or not worthy of being their friend. My romantic relationships have, without doubt, been affected by my downfalls. Even if everything is great, I will become suspicious and worry about them leaving. I have a hard time trusting men that I am involved with and the women in their lives. I believe I think this way because I have never understood how my dad, who was married and had four healthy children, could up and leave us for, not just any woman, but my mom's best friend.

Impact on Clinical Work

When it comes to clinical work, I am worried about my clients thinking I am not doing a good job and then they will not come back. I want to be an insightful therapist, I want patients to leave and say, "I feel so much better" and I am afraid that may not happen. If I do not begin to believe that I am capable of being a great therapist, I know I will find myself sitting in sessions worrying about it while the clients are telling me their story.

We ask the trainees to submit the signature theme paper to us four days before their presentation to give us sufficient time to review and analyze it. We, the facilitators, review the signature theme paper to identify the areas to be focused on during the presentation. We try to get a deeper sense of what the trainee is struggling with. Our goal is to put together a plan on how to help the trainees get more clarity regarding their theme, and what they can do to manage it more effectively in their personal and professional lives. During the signature theme presentation, we sit with the trainees and ask them to speak about the theme so we can get more of a feel for what it means to them. We ask questions to help the trainees build a coherent narrative of their signature theme, how it evolved and how it currently impacts them personally and professionally. We especially want them to gain a deeper awareness of and be in touch with how their signature theme may affect their clinical work, and how to turn it into an asset in therapy.

Trainees' understanding of their signature themes usually evolves during their presentations. At times, trainees identify a function of their signature theme rather than the theme itself as the dominant theme. For example, trainee, "Mary," may state that her signature theme is "needing to be perfect" whereas the core issue is her fear of abandonment. She might think that if she is not perfect, people she cares about will abandon her. With the help of the facilitators, Mary will hopefully gain some new insight about her core issue. We are particularly attentive to treating whatever issues trainees present as within the range of what people *normally* struggle with. We are looking to help them become more comfortable recognizing and being in touch with their issues when viewing themselves in the context of their clinical work. We also aim to relate to their personal struggles in ways that enable the observing students to identify and empathize with the presenter—preparing them to do the same with their clients, however they and their issues may differ from their clients.

After the completion of the presentation, we ask for the group's feedback on how they relate to what their classmate has presented. At this time, the group provides empathy, validation and support for the presenting trainee; they take turns speaking of their own life experiences, beliefs and emotions that came up for them as they listened. The group's feedback is meant to be helpful for the presenting trainee to reduce the feelings of isolation and shame. The group members also have an occasion to reflect privately more deeply about their own issues from what they hear of the facilitators' discussion with the presenter. The observers often report having gained more for themselves from the presenter's discussion than they did from their own presentations because they were not on the "hot seat" and could reflect with a clearer head about their own issues.

The Case Presentation

The second task in the POTT training is to present on a case that the trainees are working on, describing how their signature theme and other person-of-the-therapist factors (e.g. family history, gender, race, culture, etc.) play out in their work. The primary goals of this task are for trainees to have the experience of exploring and recognizing how their own personal selves and specifically their signature themes were triggered by the client family and its issues, and how their person with all that they bring to the therapeutic process influences how they relate, assess and intervene with families.

For this presentation, we strongly encourage trainees to submit a video of one of their sessions so we can help them recognize their personal selves in the technical process of conducting therapy. Trainees are also asked to write and submit a summary of the case in preparation for their presentation, focusing on their signature theme, therapeutic use of self when working with this case, information about the client and the context their work is embedded in, the client's focal issue and their hypothesis on the roots and the dynamics of the client's issue. Below are the specific questions trainees are asked to answer when preparing for their presentation:

1. State your current understanding of your signature theme.
2. Provide identifying information about the client/family (pseudo-names, ages, gender, occupation).
3. Attach the client's genogram and your own genogram.
4. State the agreed upon issue the client is seeking help for in therapy, and note anything in it that carries personal meaning for you, especially in relation to your signature theme.
5. Describe other agencies and professionals involved with this client/family and your relationship with them.
6. Describe your personal reactions to your clients, and theirs to you, connecting your signature theme to how you relate to, assess and intervene with your clients.
7. Address whatever cultural or spiritual values of yours may be coloring how you view the issues they are presenting as distinct from your client's perspectives.
8. How are the differences and similarities of the social locations of you and your clients coming into play in your relationship with your clients and your understanding of the case?

9. Explicate your hypotheses about the roots and dynamics of the client's issue.
10. Explain your therapeutic strategy with the case.
11. Identify your personal challenges working with this client around the focal issue, noting especially if your signature theme plays a part in the nature of the challenge.
12. Discuss your plan for meeting your personal challenges in this case, noting especially whether your own personal life experience can be a potential resource in dealing with this challenge.

The facilitators review the case write-up before the presentation and identify the ways they believe they can help the trainees gain insight into their personal attitudes and behavior in the context of their work with family they are presenting, and how they may purposefully use themselves to attain their goals in this therapy. During the case presentation, trainees show a segment from their video to the two facilitators so the facilitators can help identify the trainees' personal thinking, demeanor and non-verbal messages when working with their clients. The primary focus is on the work that the trainees have done with their clients so far, their therapeutic goals and the interrelationships between the personal and technical challenges they faced when trying to meet those goals. Following the class, trainees are expected to re-write the case presentation paper including the insights that they have gained from their presentations, as well as their ideas about how they plan to meet the challenges they face both with their clients and their issues.

Role-Plays

Students have a second option for an exercise to explore the use of themselves in their clinical work—the role-play, particularly if they had already had a presentation based on their paper (see Appendix B.3). Their fellow students volunteer to portray the clients, who can be any combination of people—friends, siblings, couples, families, etc. The instructors supervise the process, interrupting the student who plays the therapist at critical moments, to ask the student to reflect on what he/she is thinking and feeling at that very moment about the clients, and what he/she wants to do with it.

There are two versions of the role-play from which the students can choose. The first scenario is of walk-in clients to a clinic whom they are assigned to engage, identify their issue, develop a hypothesis about the underlying dynamics and explore their readiness to commit to a way of beginning to work on their issue. The instruction to the players is that they are to decide ahead of time their gender, age and relationship as the clients. They are not to discuss the issue they are presenting, instead coming up with something independently of one another and developing extemporaneously their relationship about whatever they come up with. The idea here is for the "clients" to base their relationship in their roles on their actual personal reactions to one another as they negotiate the focal issue and its underlying dynamics—something that the "therapist" will experience as real. The second scenario is based on a case the student is currently working on in his/her practicum, and about which the student intends to explore approaches to the client problem. In this situation, the student prepares the client-actors about the issue and the relationship dynamics of the client couple or family before the clinical session begins. The discussion after the role-play will focus on the student's signature theme and how it manifested itself in all aspects of the process they had with the clients—relationship, assessment and interventions. This is meant to be a training experience on recognizing and being in touch with what the student therapist personally experiences in the role of therapist, and how to use those insights in deciding how to actively use self in the therapist role.

Simulated Therapy

The next step in the POTT training, the simlab (simulated therapy) experience, aims to help trainees experience the impact of their signature theme in action. During the simlab sessions, trainees conduct therapy with a client family as the facilitators observe in a nearby room through an observation mirror or closed-circuit TV so they can supervise live. The classmates watch the session from yet another room through closed-circuit TV. The client family consists of trained actors who act as family members.

Each trainee gets to work with the family for one session picking up from where the previous therapist ended. From session to session the family members act as though they have been receiving therapy from one and the same therapist. Before the session, the facilitators check in with the trainee-therapists about their concerns about working with the client family. We ask the trainees to reflect on their signature themes and anticipate possible challenges. We may provide them with some feedback on how to use their signature theme in the session. However, our usual coaching consists of encouraging them before they enter the session to try to be personally present with the family, and look to connect with them before worrying about doing anything else. We want them to relax so they can have as much of their selves available to themselves when they engage with the family. The simlab experience provides an opportunity for the trainees to use all of who they are along with their signature themes as they look to connect with all members of the client family, assess the emotional needs of each member and their relationships, develop therapeutic goals, and intervene to enable the family to have a new and positive experience in the session. We aim to help the trainees have a successful experience of integrating their personal selves with their professional selves.

The simlab experience can be intimidating to the trainee-therapist. We emphasize before the session that we are there to help and not to judge, and that we will help them get through the experience and learn what they can from it. We supervise so as to emphasize an awareness of themselves in the process, and to facilitate their finding ways of successfully connecting to, understanding and providing an experience that feels helpful to the families. We want the trainees to have a positive experience of themselves in this first effort of being supervised live.

During the session we communicate with the trainees through an ear bug. We also usually call the trainees out three times during the session. A few minutes in we call out the trainees to discuss their first impressions of what is going on in the room, and help them formulate a plan for the session. Halfway through the session, we call the trainees out to assess how the session is going and suggest courses of action if there is a need to modify the plan. A few minutes before the end, we call out the trainee to discuss how to end the session leaving the clients with a clear sense of what was accomplished and how to proceed from there.

Almost immediately after the session the trainees meet with the client-actors to get feedback from them about how they each experienced the trainee connecting with them, and what they found most helpful and least helpful about the session (see Appendix C.2 for simlab feedback and questions for the therapist). The actors have also been instructed to remember that this is a first experience for these trainees, and that the trainees need encouragement from them.

After completing this live experience, trainees return to the class to get feedback. Their classmates are directed by the facilitators to be supportive of the trainee, and to offer some thoughts about what the experience of watching the session brought up for themselves about their own work with families. Every session is videotaped.

Trainees write a paper about their experience following the simlab session (see Appendix C.3 for the simlab paper guide). We ask the trainees to answer certain questions about their current understanding of their signature theme, information about the client family and their impressions about their therapeutic use of self. We then ask about the trainee's therapeutic use of self in that experience:

1. What was triggered for you personally (emotionally and/or values-wise) in this session in the relationship with the clients? In dealing with the clients' issues?
    (Here is where you identify what you are personally *experiencing* in your interactions with your clients, particularly as related to your signature theme.)
2. What did you draw from your own personal life experience and worldview in this session in relating to your clients? In dealing with their issues?
    (Here is where you describe how you made *use* of yourself and your inner process to empathize and connect with your clients, to both identify with and differentiate from them, and to actively and purposefully assess and intervene.)
3. How did this case challenge you in relating, assessing and/or intervening with your clients, and how did you deal with the challenges?

Below, a brief excerpt from a trainee's simlab paper offers an example for writing a simlab paper.

Current Understanding of the Signature Theme

Currently, I believe my main signature theme is the fear of abandonment. However, a big portion of this is my need to please others. I feel very uncomfortable thinking about others thinking poorly of me.

Information on the Simlab Client Family

The family that I saw in the simulation lab consisted of a husband and father, Alex, his wife, Margaret, and their daughter, Alexandria. This middle to upper class family is a Caucasian family that lives in Villanova, Pennsylvania. They moved to the area within the past year after Alex received a job offer too good to turn down. Alex promotes a pharmaceutical drug and travels around the world selling it. He stated that this job would only be for a year or two. However, he is never home due to his job and it puts stress on the family. Margaret used to be a singer but now is a stay-at-home mom taking care of her 18-year-old daughter, Alexandria, who is in her senior year of high school where she attends an all-girl school in Villanova. It appears Alexandria has had the most trouble transitioning to their new life in Pennsylvania.

The family was referred to therapy due to the struggles Alexandria is having in school. Alexandria started not having many friends at school and tends to cut school. When the family first started coming to therapy they believed this was the main issue. They were seeking help to get Alexandria back on track. However, over the weeks they began to understand that their family is very disconnected, and each one of them is struggling and feels alone. As the therapist, I observed this loneliness and need for connection in each family member.

Therapeutic Use of Self

I could understand how difficult it must have been for Alexandria to up and move from the only place she ever knew. The worst part was that she was in her last year of high school. I did not feel anyone had really discussed with her how hard that must have been. I was hoping that by doing this, she would feel like I understood her and she could open up to me more. For Alex, I wanted him to understand that I understood that he was doing this all for his family, even if it was not turning out the way he had planned. I validated how difficult it must be for him that he works so hard to provide a comfortable life for his family but when he comes home, he does not feel he is a part of the family. With Margaret, I tried to make sure she knew I understood that she was alone most of the time and that she left everything she knew behind as well. Throughout the session, I tried to ask each one how they felt when another family member would say something. My hope was that they would better understand one another realizing they are all seeking the same thing, to be loved and connected.

Their class and race did not make me feel uncomfortable. I was uncomfortable with working with an 18-year-old female who is outspoken. I was nervous she might get angry and yell at me so I tried my best to connect with her most of the session. I find that I am always uncomfortable beginning a session with a male, if he is the father. For Alex to state immediately that he has had better days, I thought the session was going to be all downhill from there. I am still trying to understand why I get uncomfortable initially working with fathers, but I would have to connect it to the relationship with my own father.

The Last Task: Final Reflection

After completing the year-long POTT training, trainees are asked to write a final "reflection" paper with the purpose of thinking about the effect on them of the process they have been through, focusing on their personal and professional growth, as well as providing their feedback about the training. Below are the questions in this paper (see Appendix C.4 for a guide to the final reflection paper):

- **Personal change**: Reflecting on the process you went through this year, how has the view of your signature theme changed? What personal changes have taken place in you and in your relationships as a result of the experiences that you had in this class?
- **Professional growth**: Reflecting on the process you went through this year, how have your clinical practice and your perception of yourself as a therapist changed as a result of the experiences that you had in this class? How do you see your clinical skills improving with respect to relationship with clients, assessment and intervention?
- **Feedback about the training**: What about the training was helpful for you in your process? What would you have wanted to be different in the training?

The final reflection paper is an opportunity for the trainee to articulate and appreciate their growth, understand where they currently feel stuck and set goals to improve their therapeutic use of self for the future. A final example is provided below from the same trainee's paper.

Personal Change

I have realized through this process that my experiences are very real and that they matter. I no longer have to get over them or force myself to feel guilty that other people have bigger problems. You have taught me that they can be a part of me and I can use them to benefit my clients and myself. I know that I still have a way to go but that is okay. As long as I keep moving forward is all that matters. I have spent so much time criticizing myself for not fixing my problems already that I forgot to recognize the progress I have already made. They may be small accounts of change, but it is still change. I spoke up to my on site supervisor and was honest about how I felt about her, I have spoken up to my boyfriend (a little, still working on it), and I am still struggling with my dad. However, I have made progress with him and when he hurt me in December, I stood my ground and made sure he knew what he did wrong.

Professional Growth

I feel I have grown so much this year professionally compared to who I was. I can remember my first session where I sent the family home after they signed their consent forms because I was so afraid, to now, where I have 13 clients and work with all of their families. POTT has helped me to be less critical of myself, which helps me be less critical of others. I try to see my clients as people who have struggled through different experiences like I have and they only want to try to be better people for it.

Simlab had me a nervous wreck, not so much because I had to provide therapy to a new family, but more because I was afraid my cohort would look at me as a failure. However, simlab, with your help, made me realize what I am capable of doing. Often, I allow my own fear and thoughts to get in the way of what I can accomplish. Throughout my presentations and even others' presentations, I have become more in touch with the things I need to still work through, but also what I can use to connect to my clients. I believe I am very capable of connecting to my clients and getting them to feel they can trust me. I know I need to continue working on how to push myself to take risks and help my clients to process their own experiences without fearing they will quit therapy or get mad at me. I honestly believe my intuition is spot on most of the time. It is just that I often ignore it or put it off for a later time. If I could just start to listen to myself more, I know I would be able to help myself and others in an amazing way.

Feedback about the Training

This class, for me, has been such an important part of this process. The entire process has helped me develop more personally and professionally. I felt I learned more about myself and ways that could help me process my own experiences more. I thought it was helpful to understand the other students and be able to connect with them on a deeper level. What was even more helpful was to realize that my situation is not unique, that everyone struggles and has pain they need to work through. Seeing this in my cohort has helped me to connect more to my clients as well.

I found that I struggled with the process portion of the class after people presented. I feel part of it has to do with confidence and the other part is that I need time to process. I think I would have felt more comfortable being given the option to talk or not to talk after the presentation. However, I know I need to get more comfortable with the uncomfortable. The only other thing I would want to be different about this class would be that it is a two-year class instead of just the first year of the program. I feel our program emphasizes the use of self so much and it takes more than three quarters to process our own life experiences and then how to incorporate that into our sessions with our clients.

Conclusion

This chapter offers a detailed description of the work that we do during our training. It describes the main components and the structure of each assignment and uses the papers of one trainee to illustrate and clarify the process. In the next chapter we will get deeper into the experience of this training by describing the journaling process trainees go through and how it facilitates their growth as clinicians.

References

Aponte, H.J., Powell, F.D., Brooks, S., Watson, M.F., Litzke, C., Lawless, J. & Johnson, E. (2009). Training the person of the therapist in an academic setting. *Journal of Marital and Family Therapy, 35*, 381–394.

Aponte, H.J. & Winter, J.E. (2013). The person and practice of the therapist: Treatment and training. In M. Baldwin (Ed.), *The use of self in therapy* (3rd ed., pp. 141–165). New York: Routledge.

Lutz, L. & Irizarry, S.S. (2009). Reflections of two trainees: Person-of-the-therapist training for marriage and family therapists. *Journal of Marital and Family Therapy, 35*, 370–380.

3 Journaling in POTT

Christian Jordal, Renata Carneiro and Jody Russon

Introduction

Journaling is a thread that ties together all aspects of the POTT model. As described in Chapter 2 of this book, at Drexel University we incorporate the POTT model into the master's level curricula via a series of sequential courses, occurring in the fall, winter and spring, over the first year of our master's degree program of study. One consistent assignment across all three courses is a weekly journal that students maintain to reflect on what they are learning from their class experiences about their personal selves in the context of their formation as therapists. The POTT model then expects students to focus their journals on the use of this self-awareness to actively, positively and purposefully use themselves, with whatever their personal issues, as a therapeutic tool.

The journal assignment is more than a means to monitor the students' participation and engagement in their classes; it is a means to emotionally "hold" the students over the entire series of courses, as they confront their personal selves, wrestle with identifying and accepting their signature themes and manage the challenge of using their newfound knowledge about themselves in their clinical work. They are encouraged to be open and vulnerable in their reflections to the best of their ability. Further, the journal assignment reinforces the oral feedback given by the two course leaders to students during their class presentations. It is important to reiterate to students that this assignment is not a traditional reflective journal, where a stream-of-consciousness thinking is often sufficient. Rather, students are guided via feedback to their journal entries in how they apply their expanding understanding of themselves to their development as clinicians.

Format of Journals

Basically, in their journals, students consider the following: (1) how to address their own identification and differentiation with the other students' signature themes as they would to clients' presentations of their personal issues; and (2) how to connect their experiences in class related to their signature themes to the work they are doing with clients. Students are being prepared to practice using this newfound self-awareness in building relationships, assessing and intervening with their clients. Although the grading structure changes over the three terms, the process of submitting journals remains the same. In the first term, students are directed to submit journals by a pre-determined time, typically three days after the previous class. We review student journal entries each week and meet to discuss our understanding of the entries to build consensus for the feedback. This feedback is then relayed to each student individually before the next class meeting.

The focus of the journal entries during the first term is basic concepts. Students identify one or more personal signature themes for themselves, which they present in class. These themes reflect what they consider to be core struggles and personal challenges, which they anticipate will manifest in various ways in their clinical work. The journal structure allows students after class to give further consideration to their personal issues via what came up for them personally in the class presentations. Students are guided to reflect on their personal reactions to class content as they might on reactions to clients in clinical practice. In the winter term students begin to directly relate what they have learned about their signature themes to their clinical work by presenting videotaped excerpts of their clinical work or engaging in spontaneously improvised role-plays in which they assume the role of therapists to clients played by fellow students.

During the spring term, students journal in detail about what they experience as they or their colleagues try actively and purposefully to use themselves to assess, intervene and build relationships with simulated clients, played by paid actors, in a simlab. As described in Chapter 2 of this book, the simlab is a multidisciplinary training environment, historically used within medical healthcare fields, as a medium to test and train student skill development using artificial mannequins and actors playing simulated patients. With our students we offer a live supervision experience paying special attention to their use of self in the clinical process. The feedback we offer after the live supervision includes prompting to relate what they are learning in this experience to their clinical work in their actual clinical placements. Note: Master's degree students begin their clinical placements in the fall of their first term in our full-time program. We capitalize on the importance of students utilizing their personal selves within their clinical roles to their work with clients by requiring students to provide a clinical example of their use of self in their journal every week in the spring term.

Journal Grading

There are many ways to incorporate journaling into the POTT program. Here we describe how we built it into the curriculum at the Couple and Family Therapy program at Drexel University (the entire program, step-by-step, is described in Chapter 2). In the Drexel program journal submissions encompass 25 percent of the POTT grading structure per academic term. Students are required to journal every week, as soon as possible after the end of class, when the reactions to and memories of the class presentations are still fresh in mind. We give a deadline for journal submission approximately three days after the class prior. With this said, students should have a journal entry for every POTT class over the series of the three terms (i.e. 30 total journal entries).

Evolution of Grading Criteria

The grading of journal content deepens to match the student's immersion in the model. It is also reflected in the amount and depth of feedback provided. The fall term guidelines require students to weave class content with their personal reactions. The goal is to expose students to experience the dual process of the POTT model. This means that students start learning how to filter their classmates' life experiences through their own personal experiences while at the same time developing the ability to reflect on and manage their reactions in ways that make it possible for them to use both their insights and emotions to inform and enrich their clinical activities. This dual process allows students to explore and expand on the use of their own signature themes in their clinical tasks.

Journaling guidelines for the winter term direct students to connect their signature themes to their clinical work. For class they can take turns writing up cases, focusing on particular issues and encounters with clients that present clinical challenges to them involving personal issues of their own. Students are then asked to present a videotaped clip of 10–15 minutes that illustrates the point of their focus. We guide students to search within themselves for experiences and feelings that facilitate a deeper connection and understanding of their clients' experiences to facilitate intervening in ways that most effectively reach their clients. Alternately, students also have the option of participating in a supervised clinical role-play. In this option, two or three other students volunteer to simulate a couple or family that walks into a clinic off the street asking for a consultation. The student scheduled to present takes on the role of intake worker, and attempts to engage them in identifying their issues and working to decide whether and how to address their issues. We stop the action periodically to ask the "therapists" to reflect on what they observe of the clients, what they make of it, what they personally experience in reaction to the clients themselves and their issues and then what they want to do with all that information. The emphasis is on the therapist integrating self-reflection with clinical thinking. At the end of the role-play (40 minutes), the "clients" provide feedback to the "therapist" about how they experienced him/her, and then so do the other students who served as audience (15 minutes). We attempt to make a positive experience for the student "therapist," guiding the self-reflection and clinical action, so that the student can learn something about using self-reflection in a clinical encounter. The journaling that follows both for the presenter and the rest of the students is to focus on their own personal reactions to the experience and how it might translate for themselves into self-reflection in a clinical context.

This self-reflection is a primer meant to prepare the students to think about how they will be able to actively and purposefully use their personal reactions and associations to enhance their clinical performance.

Finally, in the spring, students get a chance to apply all of what they have learned through a supervised experience working with simulated patients. They will attempt to use the POTT model to purposefully incorporate the use of their personal selves with their clinical training to connect, assess and intervene with a client family. Students are then expected to journal about the clinical event; whether they were the one supervised or were observing through closed-circuit TV. They are to speak to the clinical process with an emphasis on how the supervised student used the self in the process, and what this meant to those who observed as they attempted to project themselves into the clinical encounter they witnessed.

Content grades are based on the students addressing both the personal and the clinical in their journal entry. The purpose of building the clinical example into journals is to enhance students' ability to apply the POTT model actively in their clinical placements. The goal of the journal-grading framework is to spur students to reach the point where they can readily recognize and access what they personally bring to the clinical process, and use it as a mechanism to relate, assess and intervene instinctively in their clinical work.

Journal Themes

There are several recurrent themes that students report experiencing over the course of their POTT training. These themes often evolve as the students progress over the series of the three courses. In the following section we will breakdown our experience by term, using examples to support some of the themes typified at each stage.

Fall Journal Themes

The POTT process is demystified during the fall term. Students experience some anxiety about a course that states up front that they will be exploring their personal issues. During the first couple of weeks of journal-writing, students begin to identify their personal issues while also speaking of their fears about presenting in front of their cohort about their insecurities and vulnerabilities. Generally, we have found that those who choose to become therapists come in to the POTT process with a natural inclination to pay attention to the struggles of those around them. With this said, the challenge for students' journal-writing in the first term is noticing and articulating emotional experiences surrounding those struggles. Students also puzzle about the idea that their own struggles and vulnerabilities can be assets in therapy, when what they experience is shame around having vulnerabilities and "issues" in the first place. Based on our experience working with several POTT cohorts, students' journal themes for the fall term often reflect the following: (1) demystifying the POTT process; (2) connectedness; (3) exploration of fears and vulnerabilities; and (4) beginning to articulate their emotional experiences.

Fall Journal Theme Examples

DEMYSTIFYING THE POTT PROCESS

Students usually begin their POTT experience with a myriad of feelings, notably excitement mixed with anxiety and confusion. They come in expecting to be challenged to share about their personal issues, and are ambivalent of how much they want to reveal of themselves. Managing expectations is a major theme in the beginning weeks of the fall term. The following is an example from Mandy, a POTT student, in her first journal (all names and identifying details have been changed to preserve students' anonymity):

Learning what is expected and what is to come during this course was helpful in easing my anxiety. It was nice to hear Dr. Aponte and Dr. Jordal discuss why they thought the course was so special to our program. Although I am nervous to be vulnerable and open up in ways that I haven't before, Dr. Aponte and Dr. Jordal reassured me that class is a safe space to explore those hidden areas. Hearing my classmates' thoughts about the class was also reassuring. It was nice to know I wasn't standing alone in my anxiety.

This course will force me to be more transparent than I have ever been. Normally, I do not share my insecurities with anyone, but especially not with a room full of people I don't know well. I am nervous to let others know my central theme because then my peers will hold a little piece of me. They will have access to my vulnerability. On the opposite side, I will hold a little piece of them after they share. Once I think of the presentation in such a way that as a class, we mutually hold a little piece of everyone, then I am less nervous and more encouraged.

As recognized by Mandy, we encourage exploration of expectations, as it allows students to practice connecting their perceptions of class to intrapersonal experiences. Further, this writing exposes students' anxieties and gives faculty a chance to respond personally to their fears or address their concerns in class.

CONNECTEDNESS

A common thread in the fall journals is the desire to experience connectedness with instructors and classmates. Students frequently write about the supportive atmosphere of the class, including a desire to bond and learn from each other. This interest in connection serves as a way for many students to manage their fears about the disclosure of personal information. With each journal entry they experience an immediate supportive connection to the faculty in the instructors' written responses to their concerns.

EXPLORATION OF FEARS AND VULNERABILITIES

As the fall term progresses, students begin their signature theme presentations. During this process, students tentatively approach self-disclosure and acknowledgment of personal vulnerabilities. A common theme of student presentations is struggling to make sense of family of origin experiences. Students have a range of reactions to the content presented in class by others and produce journals indicative of where they are as they process their own family experiences. In her journal, Jacqueline speaks to her vulnerabilities surrounding family of origin issues.

I feel like I am drowning in this class, despite my best efforts to stay afloat. I was so embarrassed when Dr. Jordal said that he did not understand what my signature theme even was, but truthfully, I do not know how to identify specifically what it is either. I know what I struggle with, but I am struggling to find a way to sum it up in a sentence or phrase. Dr. Jordal's suggestion that I might have built up anger towards my parents originally caught me off guard, and I wanted to refute what he said, but after processing this idea I began identifying many ways in which I am frustrated with my parents, but have never felt like I could address these problems because of all my parents have done for me. I think my parents and my relationship would be better if I was able to take them off of a pedestal and acknowledge their flaws, but I am not sure how to do that until I am able to live completely independent from them.

Next, in a later entry Jacqueline explores in depth her fear of disappointing her parents, and is able to relate that to her clinical work.

Now that I feel clarity about what my signature theme is I am able to make connections to how it has been a part of my personal relationships, especially my relationships with my parents. My fear of their disapproval has had me shackled to their desires for me and led me to make decisions for them rather than for myself. I have already seen how my awareness of my self can positively affect my clinical work. For the first time I felt a genuine connection to my client, that stemmed from my willingness to see myself in her rather than just trying to empathize with her on a superficial level.

As instructors, we take every opportunity to offer positive feedback for the triumphs students experience. In addition, many students are just learning how to acknowledge and present fears and vulnerabilities as speaking of something not shameful, but humanly universal, a message we continually emphasize. The journal-writing allows a safe opportunity to give voice to this growing acknowledgment of all aspects of the self, the dark, the light and the misty. As the journals are only shared with the course instructors, students use the journaling as a sounding board for their own processing.

BEGINNING TO ARTICULATE EMOTIONAL EXPERIENCE

Students become acquainted with the concepts of identification and differentiation in the fall term. They grasp the importance of identifying with another's struggles in life, but the concept of emotional differentiation is not as accessible to them. The idea of remaining grounded in their own sense of self and emotional experience, while empathizing with their fellow student's experience, evolves more gradually. When accessing this place of vulnerability, the tone of the journal entries tends to shift from a focus on content to a focus on students' awareness of themselves in relation to their classmates, which is intended to train their self-awareness with clients. We take advantage of the feedback process to guide the students in this process.

Winter Journal Themes

The winter term revolves around students' awareness of themselves in the role of therapist. The focus is on encouraging students to see their signature theme as it relates to their clinical work. It is common for students to view their personal issues as impediments to their work. At this stage of the training it is the principal task for us to help students view their signature themes, with all their fears and failings, as assets that help them personally resonate with their clients' stories of pain, disappointment and discouragement. Overall, students struggle to incorporate feedback they have received from class presentations and journals, specifically to slow down the pressure to problem-solve enough to stay in touch with what is going on within themselves as they attempt to apply all they are learning to *do* as therapists. We continue to focus on providing specific feedback to help students make connections between their signature theme, their clinical tasks and the personal process within the therapeutic relationship. Students' journal themes for the winter term typically reflect the following: (1) awareness of common struggles; (2) viewing signature themes as assets; and (3) shift from "doing" to "being."

Winter Journal Theme Examples

AWARENESS OF COMMON STRUGGLES

Over the course of this term, students observe clinical encounters in the case presentations and role-plays of their peers, and receive feedback on their own work. We cultivate their awareness of common human struggles and experiences, highlighting that everyone has areas of woundedness and pain. This awareness helps students to recognize parts of themselves in others, which in turn deepens their understanding of their own signature themes and how they manifest themselves in therapy. For example, in her journal, Stephanie stated how she connected with the theme of "being avoidant of feelings" presented by her classmate. She journaled about how observing another student's presentation resonated with her own experience as a clinician and a person.

I could relate to Kristy regarding the idea of being avoidant with feelings. I tend to have a constant battle with showing my emotions versus feeling my emotions. As Kristy described experiences throughout her life . . . I could not help but think of myself. While describing her painful emotions, I felt deeply saddened because I felt as if we shared similar feelings and emotions. Particularly, I tend not to express myself or become open with others due to a fear of judgment. I have found this to be true, as things have directly affected me within my family. Trying to please family members and to be seen as perfect has caused me to be avoidant with my feelings regarding times that I have felt inadequate. I have always been unsure as to how family members or friends may react if I am not performing up to their expectations. Because of this, I tend to experience anxiety about certain outcomes, which is similar to Amy's explanation of her experiences in her clinical work. I have had difficulty engaging and connecting with clients without withdrawing. When situations or experiences may be similar to mine, I withdraw because I do not want to feel the same emotions. I feel as if the moment I show emotions, I become weak, and I do not want others to perceive me as weak, especially in a professional setting. As of right now, I am unsure as to how to get a client past a similar mindset. However, I do believe that if I am more comfortable and secure with myself, then my clients will react and mirror my actions, which will allow me to better connect with them without withdrawing due to my own fear of showing emotions.

In this journal, Stephanie was able to identify a commonality between herself and Kristy: a tendency to avoid her emotional experiences. Stephanie then spoke to how this was a manifestation of her signature theme, a fear of being judged. Moreover, in her journal she shared how not being comfortable with her own emotions was problematic for her in session, much like she felt in her family of origin. Overall, Stephanie used her journaling to actively reflect on how her personal life struggles connected with those of others.

VIEWING SIGNATURE THEMES AS ASSETS

Students are encouraged to incorporate their signature theme feedback into their case presentations during the winter term. In the beginning of POTT training, students focused primarily on how their signature themes "got in the way" of their clinical practice. For example, they commonly talked about their need for control affecting negatively their ability to connect emotionally or to let the client take the lead. Students also discussed their tendency to align with the children in families because of their own conflicts with their parents.

Toward the end of the term, however, students are generally able to think of their parents as struggling with their own commonly human vulnerabilities, and through this awakening so also the parents in the families they counsel. It is at this time that they begin to understand that accessing their own personal and family struggles can be an asset to them in the therapeutic process. This realization is fostered for students while presenting and observing their case presentations, and the journaling provides another context to further reflect on this insight. The student in the next excerpt, Melissa, began her POTT process struggling with recognizing her vulnerability. In this journal, she describes an experience with a client where her ability to access her emotions served as an asset in her work.

While trying to understand the concept of assessment, it reminded me of a recent situation regarding a new client. During this particular experience, a new client arrived to take part in outpatient services regarding signs of impulse control. The identified patient who is a ten-year-old male came in for treatment with his grandmother, who is also his caretaker. Upon arrival, the client's grandmother informed me . . . about current issues within their family. During this time, the grandmother immediately began to have a mental break down, crying about her emotional state of being overwhelmed. Immediately, I wanted to sink in my chair and I could feel my eyes starting to water up. However, in the same moment I wanted to remain strong for the client as well as myself, because of a fear of being perceived as weak due to crying . . . I could feel her sense of being overwhelmed as well as the pain that she has endured while having to raise not only her own children, but her grandchildren as well. As the client discussed current stressors and the reasons behind them, I was able to realize my emotions towards the situation in order to empathize with the family. Most specifically, the client reminded me of my grandmother and certain issues that she had to deal with while being a mother to eight children as well as trying to maintain and provide for her grandchildren and great-grandchildren. By being able to connect and empathize with the client, I was able to have a better understanding of underlying issues. I was also able to experience an emotional distance, distinguishing between my experience and theirs.

SHIFT FROM "DOING" TO "BEING"

In order to feel a sense of competency, many students initially attempt to solve their clients' problems, without connecting with their emotional experiences and living stories. We use the feedback to their journals to help students slow down the process in order to foster connections with clients. The following journal excerpt provides an example of the shift from "doing" to "being" in therapy.

Elaine mentioned how she doesn't like looking at the emotional aspect of things with her clients. She said it's difficult to connect with them emotionally. I feel the same way because I fear my emotions will get in the middle of me thinking clearly. I have a client who recently had an uncle pass away. I could sense that she was sad, but I couldn't let myself also feel sad with her. I thought if I was also sad, I couldn't help her. Putting my guard down means I may have feelings that make me feel "weak" . . . Dr. Aponte said we should face it because facing the challenges will help us connect with our clients. From now on, I'm going to try to be more conscious of my own feelings . . . in order to help me understand them better. During my presentation, I definitely learned a lot. I realized that I was pacing myself way too fast. I was trying too hard to get to the end goal . . . Dr. Aponte said that the path we take with our clients wouldn't be straightforward. Dr. Jordal also mentioned that we might have to make crazy turns to get to the end goal. Now I know that it's okay to go the long way. Making short cuts only make the results temporary. By taking the long way and understanding my clients, I may learn new things and really help them. I realized that I am helping my clients at this moment even though we aren't moving in the speed I want to. From now on, I'm going to have a session goal of just trying to learn new things about my clients in order to open up new possibilities for their treatment. I'm going to try to be more patient and take things slowly in order to enjoy the journey I have with my clients.

In her journal, Sara acknowledged that she used to perceive her own emotions as a weakness. Sara saw her feelings as an impediment in the process to getting the client to move forward. Knowing that her ability to connect with others' emotional experiences was a way to build understanding, Sara made an active goal to slow down and concentrate on navigating the journey with her clients instead of for them. In the past, she had spoken about her struggle to slow down the session and her concern of not being a "good enough" therapist. It was not until the reflections of this journal entry that she fully acknowledged the benefit of being present and the experiential tools she could miss if she were not tuned in to the client's experience.

Spring Journal Themes

The journals in the spring term emphasize application. By this time the intentional use of self is an ubiquitous aim for the students. However, while there are possible typologies around growth, each student is in essence growing at his/her own pace. The foundation of the clinical application process is the increased access to themselves that the students work toward in previous terms. As described in the first chapters in this book, self-awareness and self-access are two important goals of the POTT training. The ability to move from awareness to access is facilitated by acceptance of one's own vulnerable humanity. The aim of the model is for students to realize that being able to access their own struggles is a vital part of any therapeutic process. Students better able to accept their flaws and limitations, as well as their troubled history, were better able to make this shift from awareness to access. This self-acceptance, which opens access to their own vulnerable humanity, manifested in a sense of presence with clients that allows them to feel connected to their clients' experience, and, it may be assumed, makes it more possible for clients to feel connected and heard.

Spring Journal Theme Examples

By the spring term, students are more experienced with the POTT process, having completed their signature theme and case presentations. They are ready to deepen their POTT exploration via live feedback from us on how to actively and purposefully use themselves in a case consultation format. Students generally experience anxiety about being evaluated, in the moment, by instructors and being observed by classmates. This anxiety often permeates their journals. It is important to normalize students' emotional experiences, while challenging them to continue to explore the use of self in their clinical work. Students' journal themes for the spring term typically reflect the following: (1) increased access to oneself; (2) making connections to using oneself; and (3) accepting family of origin issues.

INCREASED ACCESS TO ONESELF

Again, by the spring term, students generally demonstrate an increased *access* to self in their therapeutic work. They begin to use parts of themselves throughout the therapeutic tasks of relating, assessing and intervening with clients. Because the spring term is focused on applying what students have learned to the exercise of working with the simulated client families, the journals reflect their thoughts and reactions to the use of self in the various components of the therapeutic process. The journals give us an opportunity to respond to the students' personal reactions to a broad range of actions they and their fellows engage in with clients. We can help underline what they bring of themselves to these therapeutic tasks. The following journal excerpt represents an example of how students actively access themselves through the lens of their signature theme. For this student, Debby, this frame guided her in understanding potential next steps in her clinical work. She was well in touch with her tendency "to be controlling and attempt to rescue" when faced with a child at risk. With the help of her clinical supervisor, she was able to intervene actively without succumbing to her tendency to become enmeshed with a client family. The supervision guided her in her efforts to maintain a differentiated stance.

My signature theme of jumping to rescue was challenged this week in my practicum. I've been working on a case that is especially triggering for me, as we . . . suspect that the IP has been sexually abused. The caregivers are in a deep state of denial at the possibility. This mimics my own experience and ignites my tendency to be controlling and attempt to rescue the client, not trusting that the caregivers will or are capable. In my on-site supervision, we have been working to create a frame for use with this family. Last week, we set the stage for this musical family with a frame that suggested the caregivers and their other children were all pianos (they are expert piano players). But now though, this child (our IP) is a guitar – the caregivers must learn to play a new instrument, but they already know all the fundamentals: how to read music, keep time, etc. This week, we built on that frame by asking the family to sit in the adjoining room while I led the session from the doorway and coached . . . [them] . . . through the enactment of their negative pattern. This same communication pattern had been negatively playing out over the weekend, but with coaching . . . [they] . . . were able to be heard and come to a new understanding of one another. Using this frame allowed me to keep my distance, both physically and emotionally (by allowing me to not be triggered), and permitted the family to be connected and learn a new way to interact.

MAKING CONNECTIONS TO USING ONESELF

Similarly with the increased access to oneself, students also begin to make connections between how to use themselves in therapy and their personal experiences. For example, students often draw from their own emotions to reach out and connect with the emotional experiences of their clients. With continuous feedback from us, students start to grasp that understanding clients' emotions through their own feelings does not necessarily mean self-disclosure. Students can draw from their own experiences as a way of forming a relationship with clients without having to disclose their own analogous personal experiences. In this excerpt, Shawna reflects on the simlab presentation of another student. She establishes which parts of herself she would choose to access in order to assist herself with this case.

I think I would have been able to manage the crisis of my client discovering her ovarian cancer. By manage, I mean staying present and not trying to fix. I am good in a crisis situation in which soothing and listening are necessary instead of confrontation and questioning. My signature theme, avoidance of taking responsibility for confrontation and conflict, are not much activated when I am supporting someone who is saddened and upset. I think Macie (the student-therapist) did a great job with her body language, tone of voice, empathic statements. In dealing with the crisis I would have drawn on my father's illness and death from cancer. We did not sit on the couch crying. He did not tell me definitively he was dying. But I did sit with him on the couch and later on the bed and I know that those close moments were the only silver lining in the illness. I would have emphasized the healing power my clients demonstrated in their closeness during the session.

My sessions with my clients have not been involving death and dying but rather birth. My client's friend who is living in the household is having a baby and my client expressed sadness that she is not able to have more children due to a health condition. I almost started reassuring her that there are other ways to become a parent (again) but then stopped and was able to use my own experience of not having children to generate empathy. I even used a little therapist self-disclosure to demonstrate that I understood. I made this choice because I was having sessions with three women with totally different socioeconomic backgrounds than mine and I had just been asking them probing questions about their lives. One of them had a perturbed expression on her face when I was congratulating her on progress so I thought she might be seeing me as a patronizing do-gooder. I could feel after I had self-disclosed a few sentences that it was enough and time to get back to the topic of the clients' lives.

Here, Shawna actively understands the difference between using oneself and the intervention of self-disclosure. The exercise of actually using one's self to implement the therapeutic tasks of relating, assessing and intervening with clients presents students with examples of how specific to the particular person who does the therapy is the manner in which they use themselves. The uniqueness of the person of the therapist colors and shapes the manner in which each carries out a therapeutic task within the working process. Within the journals, the students reflect on how what they did, or witnessed another do, in the supervised session was experienced differently according to the student's own life experience.

ACCEPTING FAMILY OF ORIGIN ISSUES

As students accept family of origin narratives, and the emotional pain associated with them, they learn to accept their own vulnerabilities. By accepting their own vulnerabilities, students are able to connect with clients in new ways. For example, one student, Melody, considered how her family of origin experience would guide her in getting to know her clients' presenting concerns. Her reflections are based off of another student's simlab presentation.

I could relate to Bob's feelings of irritation with Lynn's focus on her career and her schedule. I have also had clients that kept returning to concerns that I felt were an attempt to avoid other more pressing issues; I felt irritated because I felt like it was willful even though I knew better. In watching Bob's interaction with Lynn and hearing Lynn's feedback after, I thought about how I would approach her in a future session. I think one way to do it would be to explore what her career meant to her.

In listening to Lynn, I felt that her career was fulfilling a need for her that had been unmet for a long time. It also seemed as if she was weary of always focusing on others and wanted to focus on herself, but that she felt guilty about it and so had to justify her decision to work as a way to provide and care for others. It seems in the sessions that have happened so far, Lynn hasn't really been able to express what is going on for her, again because she doesn't want to appear selfish or self-absorbed. As a woman who has been pressured to provide for others, I can relate to Lynn very much. My extended family has often told me that I am selfish because I have chosen not to have children or get married. From their perspective, I'm depriving a man of a wife and my parents of grandchildren. My parents do not see it this way, but the pressure from the extended family has been quite acute over the years. I wonder if Lynn felt similar pressures from her family and is now reacting to it. Perhaps she was resistant to Bob's suggestion to find a way to spend more time with her daughter because she feels that she has already done what was required of her as a parent. However, she might feel guilty expressing this perspective. If I were to work with this couple next week, I would explore Lynn's relationship to her family of origin and what messages she received about femininity, womanhood, marriage and career.

Through our interaction with the students in their journals, we are able to help make explicit how their growing self-acceptance is reflected in the therapeutic experiences they have and witness in the supervised sessions. By this stage of the training they often take for granted their comfort with their own issues and how this facilitates their use of self in all facets of the clinical experience. Through the journals we are able to bring to consciousness how they have changed, and how these changes have made it possible for them to bring more of who they are personally to the work they do along with their family histories, with all their experiences and values.

Summary

Journaling serves as scaffolding for students to develop their therapeutic self. Receiving consistent, supportive feedback results in students' ability to trust the POTT process and explore how to use their woundedness to greater effect in their clinical work. We acknowledge that the self-examination and application is a new skill, and emphasize that all students bring their own particular strengths, weaknesses and challenges to the therapeutic experience. Journal-writing gives students a week-by-week opportunity to process their work and receive feedback and encouragement. Furthermore, it serves as a practice ground for students to target and shape their use of self in clinical settings. Overall, the journal assignments reinforce the fact that the work on the POTT is a growing day-by-day, session-by-session process. As an ever-changing evolution is occurring for student-therapists in the context of the POTT model, the journal serves as a witness to this process, allowing students to track and build on their growth throughout that year of training.

4   Looking at the POTT Process

The Case of Lynae

Karni Kissil

In this chapter we will demonstrate the process a trainee goes through in the POTT training by following one trainee through her development in the program, from submitting the first paper, discussing her signature theme and then its application to her clinical work, journals and finally her putting it all into practice in the supervised live session with a family simulated by actors.

Lynae is a Black, African-European woman in her first year of the master's at an accredited marriage and family therapy (MFT) program. She is in her forties, divorced and has two children. Lynae is making a career change going from business administration to marriage and family therapy. Identifying information has been changed to preserve anonymity. As discussed in Chapter 2, the first assignment in the training is the signature theme paper that students write and submit to us prior to their first presentation. Below is what Lynae wrote in her signature theme paper at the beginning of the program.

My Signature Theme

I tend to be very "self-sufficient." At the root of this is the fact that I do not trust people easily. Although I'm outgoing and find it easy to connect with others, I maintain a certain reserve and distance. I do not allow people to get too close. I have high expectations of people generally in terms of personal honesty and integrity; the bar is set really high for those I consider close friends. Experience has shown that these can be superficial, throw away qualities. I am very selective as to who I allow into my "circle of trust."

My Family History

I have four younger brothers. At the age of six, my two immediate siblings and I went to live with a couple [in England where they were living at the time]. *This was a private arrangement my* [upper middle class] *parents made voluntarily. We lived in a small village in the countryside; my brothers and I were the only non-Caucasians in the village and for miles. I do not recall being told anything in advance by my parents. One minute they were there, the next they were gone.*

The summer before I was due to transition to High School (11.5yrs) we were told that we'd be going to [our native country in Africa] *for a vacation. We were excited as we hadn't seen our younger siblings whilst we had been away and had only seen our Mom twice. I was looking forward to starting at my new school with my friends after the vacation. I remember being taken to view schools. I was a little puzzled, and kept asking when we were going back to England as I had to buy my new uniform, etc. It was always "soon." The next thing I knew I was in a strict Anglican Boarding School several hundred miles away from my family.*

The first year was horrible and a complete shock, I was very unhappy. My Aunt recommended my parents transfer me to an International School which my cousins attended. She thought I'd be better suited to it as it was attended by children from expatriate and diplomatic circles. My parents led me to believe that I'd transfer the next academic year. That expectation literally kept me going and enabled me to survive the year. The summer vacation came and went. At the start of the next academic year I went back to the Anglican school.

My Hypothesis About the Significance of the Events

My parents (individually and jointly) were not honest with me at key points in my life. They would mislead or keep me in the dark about decisions or plans that directly affected me. You can only trust someone when they have been consistently honest. My self-sufficiency is as a result of these experiences. I was protective of and mothered my brothers. Boarding school can be an inhospitable place; children can be cruel and think nothing of betraying confidences, and ostracizing others. I couldn't go home at the end of the day and talk to my parents. I had to deal with my problems myself.

How I Have Tried/Am Trying to Resolve the Challenge

I have always been interested in self-help and personal growth and development. I read books, articles, meditate and reflect. I try to learn from my experiences. I have worked hard not to bear a grudge towards my parents and to see things from their perspective. My children have been kept informed of and involved in decisions affecting them—although as the/a parent I had the final say. In my need to have a voice and "be heard" I used to be very out spoken and direct but have learnt how to temper this. I'm working on my trust issues.

Person of the Therapist

I believe it is because of my experiences that I have a strong ability to empathize with others, but it has been a double edged sword. On occasion it has been to my detriment as I did not know where to draw boundaries and would find myself emotionally and physically drained. This is something I'm very aware of and know I'll have to manage so I don't burn out. My empathy has also put me in situations where I have "sympathy over ride." I would give people the benefit of the doubt ignoring red flags. I think there is some transference on my part. Other advantages include not being afraid of change or taking risks. I also have a rich "dual" heritage [growing up in two different cultures].

I came face to face with my "trust" issue during a session with a client last week. The client was explaining how she didn't trust anyone: "because I'm talking to people and seemingly open doesn't mean I trust them." I thought to myself: *"my POTT issue is staring me in the face."* *What she said resonated and I knew how to use it to move forward. My concern is how I can manage my trust issue when faced with someone who has repeatedly cheated on their partner? My professional response has to be different from the way I'd react to such a betrayal in my personal life.*

Our Preparation Before the Presentation

Lynae sent us her write-up a few days prior to her presentation in class. We, the trainers, read the paper with great care, and then discussed our thoughts about Lynae's signature theme/s. In reviewing the paper several ideas came to mind: Lynae has been seriously betrayed by the people closest to her, people who were supposed to protect her and care for her. She had to grow up quickly and take care of herself and her siblings, emotionally and physically. Having been abandoned emotionally at such a young age and with no trusted adult to comfort her, she learned to bury her feelings and became "tough." Even when she tries to help herself, she does not reach out to other people; she relies only on herself. When she writes about her difficult experiences at school, she distances herself and does not use first person form, disconnecting emotionally when talking about painful experiences. Lynae is emotionally guarded, very suspicious of other people and cautious about allowing people into her world. She does not take risks in relationships, not allowing herself to be emotionally vulnerable.

In regards to her clinical work, we believed that if Lynae would allow herself to connect to her experiences and her vulnerability, she would be better able to use more of herself to relate deeply to her clients. We planned to help Lynae increase her awareness of the consequences of her childhood history, and of the mechanisms she uses to protect herself from feeling the emotional pain that was so unbearable when she was a child.

Lynae's Signature Theme Presentation

Lynae's next step in the program was to present her signature theme. The presentation took place in the classroom. Lynae was sitting in the front of the class, facing us, the two instructors: Harry Aponte (HJA) and Karni Kissil (KK). The presentation takes place in front of her cohort, who are observing quietly until the end of the presentation, when they are expected to provide feedback. Below are some excerpts from Lynae's signature theme presentation. We provide our reflections and describe how we worked with Lynae in the parentheses between the sections.

HJA: *Get us started.*
LYNAE: *Huh how? Well I just start talking?*
HJA: *Just focus us on what you want us to focus.*
LYNAE: *Oh well okay. I think my signature theme is my kind of like self-sufficiency and could be aloofness and kind of emotional reserve I think. And it's when I say*

> *I have that it is about not trusting people. I think I want to qualify in that I operate from the basis that I give everybody trust and there are levels of trust. And I have gone from kind of . . . let's say you have got a scale of trust from one to hundred percent. In the past I used to give everybody hundred percent trust and as they did things, they would then lose trust points. That's the only way I can describe it. And what I have realized is that actually not everybody warrants hundred percent trust because now I give people the benefit of the doubt. So what I do now is that everybody starts off with maybe ten points of trust out of a hundred and then make assumptions about how trustworthy they are. I don't automatically assume that they are trustworthy. Does that sort of make sense?*

We usually start by asking the trainees to tell us what they consider to be their signature themes. We try to help them from the very start create a coherent story around their theme and to own their experience. The way trainees talk about their signature themes also gives us an indication about how comfortable they are allowing themselves to be vulnerable, going to their dark places. In this example, Lynae stays in her head and describes her well thought out method of emotionally protecting herself. We get the impression that it is easier for her to stay in the area of her strengths and resilience than in any vulnerable emotions or painful experiences.

KK: *Impressive.*
HJA: *You don't put yourself in their hands?*
LYNAE: *Yes, yes. Exactly.*
HJA: *They may be nice people but I will not put myself in their hands until I know them better.*
LYNAE: *Yes, yes. I am more protective of myself.*
KK: *You have built up a whole model and a theory of how to protect yourself.*
LYNAE: *Probably, I think I tend to rationalize things a lot. I think things through a lot. I mean as a child I used to read books a lot. I can read lots of books very, very quickly. I have always been that way and I have always liked books because of their escapism. So I kind of tend to think things through, and I am very aware of what I am thinking, and how I'm feeling and stuff. I do process things. I don't necessarily rationalize them away, but I do try to understand. The way I learn about things is kind of like I need to excavate the foundation, then build the foundations and then go onto things . . .*

Lynae stays at an intellectual level and we want her to go deeper into her experience to connect to the emotional realm of her awareness.

KK: *What did you escape from?*
LYNAE: *I think being on my own or being on my own and not having freedom I was very much, was told what to do as a child and I wouldn't be told what to do. You can ask me to do something. You can suggest, not tell me so I kind of escaped into . . . the kind of books I read were really about children having created their own*

little societies and doing what they wanted to do . . . if *I* think about . . . *I* have never thought about it before but that is what they were. They were about children having adventures.

KK: Children having power and choice?

LYNAE: Yes, yes because *I* never had that as a child.

KK: Because reading this [the paper] it was like you were up and moving between continents and not even knowing how long it is going to take, how long *I* am going to be there. *I* have two parents one day, the next day *I* have no idea why *I* was transferred to another place, totally helpless with controlling what is happening in your life.

        . . .

LYNAE: . . . *So* there was five of us and the youngest two were twins. And then the twins weren't like six months old or something like that, and *I* remember that my mom told my brothers, the two siblings and *I* immediately behind me, that we were going to [country of origin] to see our dad and *I* thought it was a holiday. *I* just remember being very excited, and then the next thing, so one minute we were on the plane and then next minute *I* remember being at a uncle's house for maybe a few days. *I* don't know how long my mom was there . . . the next thing my mom wasn't there and the next thing my brothers and *I* were in a car . . . the next thing we were in a strange house in another place, and one minute my dad is kind of standing there and the next minute he is gone and it's just my two brothers and *I*.

KK: So you were dropped in somebody else's house?

LYNAE: Yeah.

Lynae is starting to tell her story. The connection with her signature theme is unfolding. From the way she describes the events we sense the chaos, confusion and lack of control she experienced as a little girl.

KK: *I* just wondered as a girl what did you tell yourself? How did . . . what story did you tell yourself to make sense that you were abandoned?

Although Lynae did not use the word "abandoned," this is what I felt listening to her story. I felt that in a way she lost both of her parents the day she was dropped off at her uncle's house without any explanation. Going back to my own personal experience of losing a parent I felt a strong sense of abandonment. I purposefully used this word to see if Lynae will resonate with it.

LYNAE: Well, the thing is that *I* remember sitting on the floor with my brothers and we were sitting in a circle and we were . . . *I* think this must have been shortly after my parents seemed to disappear. And *I* was talking to them in our tribal language, and because we were dual language and *I* think *I* was trying to reassure them that everything was okay or something like that, we were all together and everything and then so *I* can see us now . . . and we were sitting in a circle and *I* was talking to them, but at some point *I* got a call or message from my dad because the couple *that was looking after us phoned my dad and said that she keeps speaking to them in the tribal language and we don't understand what she is saying. So they were being excluded from these conversations and I was clearly giving my brothers instructions. They could tell that I was giving my brothers instructions and they did not have the full control because they didn't know . . . I think maybe they were asking us to do things, and they would look at me and I would say yes go ahead and it was clear to them that I was giving my brothers instructions and stuff and so we were told not to speak in our tribal language anymore so I couldn't speak to them without being overheard.* [crying] *I'm sorry.*

Lynae is going deeper into her experiences, and we understand a little more about the development of her theme. Caring for her brothers and forming a coalition with them which excluded their caretakers was a way for her to feel some control over her life. Feeling responsible for her siblings' wellbeing seemed to have helped her cope better with the helpless feeling of abandonment. When this was taken from her and they were not allowed to talk in their tribal language anymore, this is when she felt the full impact of the abandonment. Talking about these experiences is very difficult for Lynae and she can no longer stay in her head. She connects to the vulnerable feelings of that painful childhood experience.

KK: *It's okay.*
LYNAE: *I have just never spoken to anybody, and there are people who know me who don't even know this so . . . I . . . The thing that just made me cry now was because my name is [name] and that is what I have always been called. But when we went there because they couldn't pronounce my name there was a middle name which I was never called by and I was starting to be called by that name and so my identity was taken away as well* [crying]. *So I was being called by a name that wasn't mine and when all . . . that name only exists on my birth certificate. As soon as I was old enough to fill out forms for myself I only used my first name and I only realized this when I was writing this. And when anybody asks if I have a middle name, I don't have a middle name. I do but I don't because I am trying to disassociate. I was being called a name that wasn't mine and like I said last week there was a girl that this family had looked after before that had that name so it wasn't even the full middle name. So it was an abbreviation of the middle name so I was being called a name that I had never called before and then I was then being compared to somebody who had that name. So it was as if my identity was being obliterated and it wasn't me. So I think I have very strong issues around my identity and that's why if people ask me where I am from I'll tell them I am from [country of origin] and if they ask me what my cultural heritage is I will tell them that [country]. But you can't tell me who I am. And I haven't ever realized that, that is because of those identity issues.*

Lynae describes the magnitude of her losses. Not only her parents were gone, but she was stripped of important parts of her identity; she was not allowed to speak in her first language and she was given a name that she did not experience as her own. She experiences all these losses by the people who were supposed to take care of her. She counters the experience by forcefully asserting the identity of her choice—her mother tongue and land.

KK: *I think that the thing that came up to me when I read that you said that, what I wrote at the top [of her paper] is "betrayal."*

LYNAE: *Yes. That's why I . . . yeah.*

KK: *Like on so many levels you described experiences in school, the experiences with your parents. There is so much betrayal that it is not surprising that you have to build this model and theory of "how am I ever going to allow myself to trust people and where do I start." So how does it feel walking in the world with that stuff?*

LYNAE: *Well the thing is that, I think at some point, I don't know when, I just decided that I would try to be the best person I could be. And that's why I say I don't judge people. I don't. When I meet people I don't ask them personal questions about themselves apart from their name. If people ask me personal questions about me I will answer them to a point but I don't ask people personal questions about themselves. I don't ask them, are you married? Do you have kids? I don't ask anybody any of that because I just deal with the person as who they are. If we start talking and things come out then I will ask them things if it's part of the conversation. But as a "who are you and where is your place in the world?" I don't do any of that. I just literally relate to the person as I am seeing them. So I think at some point I made the decision at some point that I couldn't allow myself to be an angry person or a hurt person because that would affect the quality of my life. So I tried to kind of relate to people and then relate to them based on the quality of the relationship. It would depend on what happens between this kind of thing or the infraction.*

Lynae is giving a good description of how she consciously decided to bury her feelings and not let her history detract from the quality of person she chooses to be in the present.

KK: *So where did the hurt and anger go? What did you do with it? Like you made a decision I am not going to let this affect my life.*

LYNAE: *I think I made that decision in boarding school because I couldn't . . . At the end of the day when something happens to you, especially as a kid at school, it is nice to go home and to be with your family no matter how dysfunctional that family is, they are your family. So you know it is nice to go home and be with people that have something to do with you. Either they are related to you by blood or they are people supposed to care take you so they have some kind of responsibility for you but . . .*

Notice how the intensity of the conversation shifts when Lynae switches from a subjective first person account to second person pronouns. She does not talk about her personal experience anymore. She is distancing herself, probably from some very painful feelings.

HJA: *I'm sorry. I missed what you last said.*

LYNAE: *I said it's nice to go back to a place that is like your home base where you either have people that are related to you by blood or they have some responsibility to care take for you. So they are kind of your parental . . . your family structure. But when you are in boarding school your family is like the people in your dorm. And I don't know if anyone has ever watched or read the book, "The Lord of the Flies," but boarding school can be like "The Lord of the Flies."*

When Lynae mentions "The Lord of the Flies," a book about chaos among a group of parentless children that ends in a murder of a kid, she gives another good indication of how difficult and painful her years there have been. We want to help her access her experience and talk about it.

KK: *You did the same thing that you did here that I noticed. It's like you kind of like talking about something that is out there and it's not personal, in that same sentence you speak of children who can be cruel and think nothing of betraying confidences and ostracizing others. Can you talk about what happened to you?*

LYNAE: *Well . . . So your family are the people in our dorm and we were given . . . And it was a girls' school, a girls' only school. So we were given a school mother. So let's say you are in the first dorm so you are 11–12 and you are in the first dorm and then your school mother is in the fourth dorm so she would be around 15 . . . And so I was given a school mother who already had one school daughter. So we were in the first dorm. And so what I think they tried to do was structure it like a family unit and then we had the matron who kind of looks after all the girls. So my school mother . . . didn't want a second school daughter and she made that very clear. So I was a misplace . . . so the person that was supposed to be my kind of like parent totally rejected me . . . So I basically went through my first and second years when you should have this person to be there to talk to. She wasn't there. I didn't have that. So that was kind of a bit difficult because I can understand what was it? You don't know me. What was it about me? Why this? So I kind of had like a surrogate school mother but it was . . . so that was kind of like. . . . So what happens as well is that. . . . So your friends are the people that you. . . . You know have to confide in somebody so you have your friends who you confide in. But what happens is that people build all sorts of alliances and things. And you could. . . . If something happens to you at school you can't go home and tell anyone . . . and then you are suddenly left to fend for yourself. So what will happen is not literally like a circle where they say fight, fight, fight, because if you fight you get suspended. And that is a shame on you and your family. But you suddenly end up in a situation where people have silently chosen sides.*

Lynae is telling the story of her time in boarding school. It is clearly very difficult for her as she shifts back and forth from first to second person pronouns. Her story provides another layer in understanding the development of her signature theme; more betrayals, abandonment and a decision not to trust anyone because of more negative experiences around trusting people.

KK: *. . . Which I was thinking about and I looked at your genogram and I saw that*
            you are divorced.
LYNAE: *Yes.*
KK: *So it is kind of like with your theme. I was little bit even surprised that you*
            managed to get married and to trust somebody and love somebody and have this
            kind of relationship. And you didn't write anything about it so I was kind of . . .
            I wonder how that fit in . . . (Lynae laughs)

After helping Lynae talk about her childhood experiences, and getting a
better understanding of how her experiences shaped her signature theme,
I shift to the present. I want to know how the signature theme impacts the
way Lynae does relationships. My question about Lynae's marriage came
from my own experiences. Going back to an experience of my own with
abandonment and mistrust, and remembering the many years it took to trust
someone to the point of getting married, I was curious about how this process
had been for her.

LYNAE: *The reason I laugh when you say that is kind of a surprise that I managed*
            to get married. I laugh because when I got married . . . I didn't walk on the
            traditional "here comes the bride" thing. Mine was "mission impossible"
            (laughter). That's why I laughed. Yeah. That was my joke, like oh my god.
            She is getting married. And the interesting thing, the person I chose to marry
            . . . I took a risk because we were not . . . economic equals. . . . And I knew
            that his character was perhaps not all it could be. Well in fact it was not
            all it could be. But he was like okay I want to get married as well and I want to
            change. And what I learned from that experience is that people wanting to change
            and actually changing are two different things. So it was yeah, an interesting
            experience.
            . . .
LYNAE: *Well I have a close-knit circle of friends and I mean I have lots of friends and*
            acquaintances but they're kind of like . . . you know several . . . you know I have
            different levels of friends . . . I'm very open with people and I do have lots of you
            know . . . I have lots of people that make me think of me . . . I'm more . . . how
            do I put this? I'm more their friend than they are my friend.
KK: *Which goes along with your theme.*
HJA: *Right. Are you seeing clients now?*
LYNAE: *Yeah.*

At the final part of the presentation we always shift the focus to the clinical
work. After helping the trainee look at her personal experiences surrounding
her signature theme and how it shapes her relationships with self and others,
we want to take a look at how the signature theme manifests in her clinical
work. During this presentation, this is the first time the trainee considers the
connection between the personal and the professional and starts reflecting on
what she brings of her personal self to the therapy room.

HJA: What I am curious about . . . in a funny way your story is completely different from [classmate who presented before Lynae] but there is a certain common element in it that is about not being able to trust other people and needing to trust yourself. And what your story is one of, at least from the reading of it, it is one of being successful at trusting yourself. Because you, at least in my reading of this, are a disciplined person. You are very much in charge of yourself. So then what happens when you are with clients, and you need to relate to their vulnerability? Can you relate to them with and through your own vulnerability?

Notice here the mentioning of another student's presentation. When we work in a group format we use every opportunity we have to help trainees experience their shared humanity with their fellow classmates. Pointing to similarities in experiences and emotions helps students reduce feelings of shame about their own vulnerabilities and negative life experiences.

LYNAE: I think . . . I mean I empathize with people a lot and one of the problems I have had in the past was over-empathizing and just being too totally . . . wanting to . . . when people were going through . . . like my instinctive thing when I hear that something is happening to someone is "Oh, what can I do to help?"

KK: To save them.

LYNAE: Yeah. That is my instinctive thing. What can I do to help? And I have had to . . . now I think that and slow down before I act, if I act at all. But in the past my instinctive thing would be to try to help this person out of this situation. So I think I would say that my danger especially in the past would have been to over-empathize to the point that maybe I could have suffocated the person in my attempt to help them. Whereas now I think, well I think I learned to do is to be concerned and to want to help the person, but I kind of go at their pace and try to offer the support at their pace and rather than at my pace. Because yeah I am disciplined with myself but I recognize the fact that how I deal with myself is . . . I can't tell people to snap out of something. Whereas for myself I allow myself a period to kind of feel bad and feel sorry for myself and eat all of the ice cream God sends and whatever. And then I snap out of it. I snap out of it because I've got to keep going.

KK: What gets triggered in you that you cannot tolerate and you really have to do something to fix that? When you see somebody in need, somebody in crisis, somebody helpless there is something there that is very strong.

LYNAE: It's their pain. It's their pain I think. I don't like to see people in pain.

KK: Where does it take you that you need to immediately do something and get out of this feeling—immediately be active?

LYNAE: I don't know really. Maybe . . . I don't know. I don't know.

KK: It comes from somewhere.

In this part of the conversation I try to help Lynae connect to her feelings of helplessness and lack of control. She can connect to her sense of strength and being self-disciplined, but struggles to connect to the underlying feelings of helplessness that she works so hard to avoid. She is having a hard time going there.

HJA: *When . . . you are in trouble or you're facing something difficult . . . you are ready to act and do something about it. And so I can readily imagine you when you see somebody in trouble that you are going to do for them what you do for yourself. And that since you are so good at doing for yourself . . . you would have the expectation that you are going to do it for them. That you are going to save them.*
        . . .

LYNAE: *In my experiences with people in my personal life, with my friends, that is something that I have realized. That is why now when something happens and I think, "What can I do to help?" I don't actually do anything. I just keep that thought.*

HJA: *But the question that I have related to is that, and it's really the same question I had with [classmate], but you are coming from a very different place, but it ends up with the same question and that is whether you are able to relate to the other person's brokenness, woundedness, vulnerability, through your own? Whether you are able to allow yourself to get in touch with your own vulnerability. You were a lonely child. You were a child who wanted somebody to take care of you, to be there for you. You don't dwell on that part of you. You dwell on what you did to solve that for yourself. . . . Whether you are able to go to those feelings when you are with a client who is experiencing that. And whether you are able to allow yourself to not only remember it up here* (points to head) *but to remember it in your* (points to heart) *. . . so that then you can feel what that loneliness is like in your client at that moment . . . what it's like for your client to feel how lovable am I? Whether you are able to do that through your own experience of that so then you . . . can get a real feel for where that person is so that you get a deeper sense of what they are up against. As you then try to understand them and come up with some kind of approach to how you can help that really helps from within . . .*

LYNAE: *It's interesting because as you were speaking I was thinking about it and I would have before sitting down in this chair I would have said yes I can get to where they are emotionally, but actually when I think about when you are speaking . . . I get them mentally and logically so I totally know what they are going through because of the logical part of me but they are not getting here and I have a shelf across my heart that basically nothing is getting there.*

Lynae is able to make the connection and acknowledge how hard it is for her to connect emotionally.

HJA: *Because there is only so much that we can understand with our heads. There is a whole other part of a person's experience that they can't articulate and that we can't see with our eyes or even hear with our ears but that we can intuit if we go through our own brokenness . . . Our vulnerability can lock into theirs as they are sharing it with us. We can lock into their experience through our own and then we can begin to feel what it is that they are going through. Often times*

> *without being able to put a word to it but then that's what allows us as a therapist to be intuitive and go a little further or a lot further then what words can ever take us. That's what I am speaking to because your training has not been to do that.*

We use the students' presentations not only to work on the particular student's issues, but also to teach the presenting student along with the rest of class the concepts underlying our approach.

LYNAE: *Yeah. Yeah. I see that is something that I would have to . . . I think in my head a lot. And although I am very aware of emotions and things like that, I think I do have a protective thing there. And so while I will be very concerned about somebody who is in a bad situation and I will want to try and help them and things like that, I am not sure that the emotional part is working. I would have said that the emotional part is working because I am concerned about them and I could understand and I see where they are coming from. I've been there, oh I can understand it but in terms of like feeling . . .*

HJA: *At that very moment . . .*

LYNAE: *Yeah. Yeah. I don't feel. I can empathize because I can understand and everything, and I can usually work out what is going on with people. I don't know whether it is my intuition picking up on the logical things, but on the emotional reading I don't think I could actually . . .*

HJA: *There are many cases that you will be able to use the skills that you have, but every now and then you will get a case that is a bit of mystery and the only way that you can intuit that mystery is by going into the dark places and through your own darkness that is in you. It's not like it isn't in you. The question is whether you can allow yourself to go back to that place and find it in you and use it.*

LYNAE: *But yeah. I totally agree with what you are saying because I think that my coping mechanism has been to kind of like cover up that emotional core. And then because if I don't, then the pain is too much for me to have moved on it. So the only way to deal with whatever was going on was to cover up the emotional thing . . .*
            . . .

KK: *I want to say something too. It was very useful for you growing up. You needed it. That was the best coping skill that you could have come up [with] and survive what you had to survive because the pain was too deep. You are not that little girl anymore. You might not need that anymore. So you might be able to use it when you need it, and put it down when you don't need it, and have some control over it because it took over.*

At the end of the presentation we want to validate Lynae's experiences. Her resiliency and strengths are good, and have been serving a purpose all these years, but in order to be an effective therapist she has to learn to also use her wealth of emotions—her triumphs.

Following the Presentation

At the end of the presentation we open the floor and ask all the other trainees to share their personal experiences and thoughts while observing the presentation. We ask them to focus on how the presentation resonated with them. We do this because we find that the trainees' empathic feedback enhances the sense of shared humanity for all of them, which hopefully also will reflect in their ability to identify more personally with their clients. At the same time, their personal reflections and those of their colleagues will facilitate their personal experience of differentiation from the presenter and the rest of their cohort, again something that should help their development as therapists who can engage deeply with a client while simultaneously observing their process with the client.

Below are some examples of the feedback trainees shared following Lynae's presentation:

Classmate #1:   *I just want to say I am really proud of you. You talked about stuff that you hadn't shared with anyone and that's awesome. I was really proud of you. We did have a lot of things in common even though we have completely different stories and your story is fascinating to me. It really was. And my parents always shared so much with me and I always was like "Why can't you just leave me alone, I don't want to know." But hearing your story and the fact that you had no control over what was going on and they didn't tell you anything. It just put me in a completely different appreciation for what I went through. And you were saying that you are too good of a friend to some people and they aren't really there for you when you need them. That's like every friend I have ever had pretty much. People just . . . I'll just give and give and give and give . . . I even bought one of my friends a laptop. She needed a laptop and I was like alright, I got it, don't worry about it. And no one would do that for me. So it was really just that, and I thought it was some interesting similarities.*

Classmate #2:   *I mean kind of reiterating what [classmate #1 name] said. I relate to you in a lot of ways and I didn't necessarily know that I would relate to somebody else that much especially as far as rationalizing and processing your emotions. I do that all the time. I am a very analytical person in a lot of ways so I know exactly what I am feeling. Okay, well I am feeling like this and just kind of process it and especially with the levels of trust I am completely there with you . . . so just to let you know you are not alone so . . .*

Classmate #3:   *The one thing I really relate to you on is like how much abandonment you went through and for you to turn out to be the person that you did. You know this incredibly warm and caring person that you are. And it's just makes me realize that . . . I have trust issues too that I won't really let people near my inside. But you adapted and coped with that so well that it makes me realize that I have a lot of work for myself to do to be able to become a better therapist.*

Classmate #4:   *Just listening to all of you actually I thought I was having my own POTT session so can I be excused next week? (laughter). No, just kidding. Something that I really connected with is that [Lynae] you were the first person that I talked to at orientation and so on and so forth. And I think that when you said that you see someone in pain, the first thing that comes to you is, is there anything I can do? And I have shared with you about the struggles I was having recently and it was the same thing you said is there anything I can do, is there anything you can do? I mean I was very touched by that but yeah at the same time don't worry it's okay . . . I kind of realized that that is a similarity whereby I know we are quick to offer but yet we have difficulty accepting, but yet we want to accept. . . . Thank you.*

Classmate #5:   *You mentioned your sense of identity and how people can't pronounce your name and which I completely understand. And I admire your strength in saying this is who I am. I know it is hard for me to say this is who I am. I mean so many times . . . I know I internalize what other people think of me so much, and I wish that I could have that strength and stance to say I am not what you think I am. I don't think that's fine and I don't agree with it. This is who I am. And I think you kind of inspired me to kind of try and take that stance and see who am I and find out my own identity and kind of tap into it.*

Classmate #6:   *A lot of what you said really resonated with me. Like not having a best friend. I know exactly what you are talking about. You have close friends, people who you will tell things to but it is kind of like I keep everybody at arm's length, like everybody in my life at arm's length. I take a little from a lot of people to get my social needs met. I'm really, really analytical. I analyze all of my emotions and so I think I will have the same thing that you do. I will have that problem going to an emotional place because up here all the emotions are safe and so like when you two were talking about that, I know that I am going to have that same exact issue.*

Tracking Progress Through Weekly Journals

Throughout the training, students are required to submit a weekly journal, following each class, writing about their experiences during the presentations they observed. They are free to address anything that came up for them during the presentations. The journals provide a great opportunity for us to sense how they are doing emotionally, to provide helpful feedback to them and to assess whether any of them are struggling and need more support. They also provide another opportunity for students to take some distance from their experience, and further reflect on their own processes while witnessing the experiences of others.

Below are a few excerpts from Lynae's journals in the weeks following her presentation that demonstrate her continued internal process (her presentation took place on October 14).

10/21—Shawna's presentation really touched me . . . I cannot fathom how parents can inflict such cruelty on their children . . . it made me think "that's why I don't allow people to get too close, no one should have that kind of power or control over another," no matter how much they supposedly "love or care about you."

10/28— . . . I realized that the last two relationships I had in the past 15 years have both been long distance. I was fine with that because it suited me. . . . Now I want a relationship with someone in the same city.

11/18— . . . Dawn's struggle to allow herself to trust someone enough to be vulnerable and allow them to take care of her, this is something that I know I have to deal with. I've gone from thinking I don't need to be taken care of emotionally to knowing that I need and want that from my partner . . . I need to work on myself so that I am able to allow myself to receive it . . . trusting someone enough to put myself in a vulnerable place.

Lynae's Simlab Experience

As discussed in Chapter 2, we use a simulated therapy experience (called "simlab") in our training. During the simlab session, a trainee conducts therapy with a client family as the facilitators observe in a nearby room through an observation mirror or closed-circuit TV so we can provide live supervision. The other trainees watch the session from another room through closed-circuit TV.

The client family consists of paid actors who act as family members. Each trainee gets to work with the family for one session picking up from where the previous therapist ended. From session to session the family members act as though they have been receiving therapy from one and the same therapist. Before the session, we check in with the trainee-therapists about their concerns about working with the client family. We ask the trainees to reflect on their signature themes and discuss possible challenges for them with this client family.

Below we describe Lynae's experience working with the clients in her simlab experience using excerpts from her write-up of the session and the session's transcript.

Here is how Lynae described the clients and their reasons for seeking therapy:

Bill (44yrs) and Meredith (45yrs) a married couple are parents to the identified patient Max (17yrs) and his sister Sarah (24yrs). Bill is a Sports Announcer, Meredith a High School Principal, Max is in the 11th grade, Sarah is a graduate student. Sarah is Bill's biological daughter from a prior relationship when he was in his late teens, early 20s. Bill and Meredith married when she was expecting their first child, Robbie, who had heart problems and eventually died at the age of four. Max was born shortly after.

The relationship between Bill and Meredith is distant, they have stopped functioning as a couple. Meredith describes them as "like two ships in the night." Meredith and Max are very close. She is very protective of him. Bill and Max's relationship is conflictual and distant. Max and Sarah are close and confide in each other to an extent. Bill and Sarah were close and remain so although she is rarely at home. Sarah and Meredith had a close relationship

*when she was younger but there appears to be some emotional distance and low-level conflict
between them now.*

*The presenting problem is Max's problems at school. He was getting into trouble with
teachers, committing acts of vandalism such as setting book bags on fire, and was having
problems with other students. Max felt that he did not fit in and wanted to attend another school.
Bill and Meredith did not know what to do with him and wanted help getting Max and "his
problems fixed." Meredith's attempts at discipline were not working and she would not allow
Bill to intercede as she felt he was too strict. Max had little to no respect for his father. There
was a clear triangle or coalition between Meredith, Max and Bill as the outsider.*

Lynae went into the session hypothesizing that the origin of the issue the family
was struggling with was unresolved grief over the death of their son, Robbie:

*I believe that the unresolved emotional issues from the loss of Robbie are at the root of the
matter. Bill, Meredith and Sarah have not fully grieved his loss as individuals or as a family.
Robbie is ever present in all their minds even if it is not overtly acknowledged. I believe that
Bill and Meredith's emotional distancing stemmed from this issue. They were both unable to
comfort each other and withdrew into themselves to try to deal with their loss. Instead of turning
to each other at an emotionally traumatic time they turned away. This also led to resentment
of the other as their failure to communicate about their loss and their "business as usual"
demeanors which they adopted as coping mechanisms gave the wrong impression to the other
that "he/she does not care, or care as much as I do."*

Before starting the session we discussed with Lynae her plan. She wanted to
help Bill and Meredith work together as a couple to parent Max, building
on the progress made in the previous session. She also wanted to address
Max's problems at school to see if they could get to the core of what was
really troubling him. Although she did not plan to bring up Robbie's death
during the session she acknowledged that she was prepared to address it if it did
come up. Prior to the session we also talked with Lynae about her signature
theme and suggested that her challenge would be to focus on being with the
parents, in particular, and connecting to them using her own emotions and
experiences.

When Lynae walked into the therapy room she found out that Max did not
show up to the session. It turned out that Max snuck out of the house the night
before and the family did not know where he was. He did not respond to phone
calls. Lynae began the session with the parents and Max's sister, Sarah. They
discussed Max's disappearance for a few minutes and the parents' efforts to be
on the same page as far as parenting Max. Sarah talked about her concern for
her brother and stated that she did not want to lose another brother.

SARAH: *To be honest this kind of pisses me off cause like they've already lost one son . . .
          I don't want to lose another one. You know? So it's kind of pissing me off that
          he's not even . . . it's one thing for a teenager to act out, but to just leave is totally
          different and that's kind of pissing me off.*

We see this as an opening to bring up the issue of Robbie's death and hope that Lynae will follow.

LYNAE: *You're saying you don't want to lose your brother again, do you . . . is the relationship with you and Max, does he listen to you, did you . . . ?*

SARAH: *Sometimes, but like not completely. I—I try, to help him. I tell him my phone's always, like it's not on silent ever. You know. Um. . . . Like if he needs me to pick him up or if he needs to talk or whatever, like it's on. You know, that's why we got cell phones, right? Um . . .*

LYNAE: *Did you, Bill and Meredith work . . . did you two work together in terms of um, disciplining Sarah when she was younger? What do you think you did then that worked but maybe changed in the way they were working with Max?*

We notice that Lynae did not follow the opportunity Sarah presented and chose to stay with the current issue. We are waiting to see if she will get back to it.

BILL: *I . . . I felt I felt like, I don't know what it is, but I, I felt more over protective with Sarah. I don't know why, whether it was sexist or whatever. Just as a girl, my little girl, I'm more concerned about her because a lot of bad things could happen to girls and women that generally don't happen to boys. Not that they can't happen to boys, but with Max, since he was a boy I tried to instill a toughness but . . . you know, get him ready for the world, cause you know kids are cruel, things like that and you gotta be able to stand up for yourself but for her, it—it was a different thing. And you know I had her when I was really young so . . . it was always when I was young I was still in school and stuff and she was a toddler still so I would be more like a big brother kind of thing for a while so I felt like an older protective brother. It's a different thing, the age gap. Max is seven years younger than her so now by that time when Max was born we'd already lost Robbie and I'm in a whole different place.*

Here we notice another opportunity to discuss the death of Robbie and how it affected the family.

LYNAE: *Okay, and, when you think back to your childhood, your family of origin, what was the . . . Did your parenting style come from there, or what was the parenting like?*

Lynae again does not follow the opening and asks about Bill's childhood memories. They talk for a few minutes about the parenting that Bill experienced growing up. Then Lynae shifts and asks Meredith about her relationship with Max, after she hears her referring to him as her "baby".

LYNAE: *Meredith, you referred to Max as your baby?*

MEREDITH: *Mhm.*

LYNAE: *So, how did that go, affect the way you kind of like . . . take care of him?*

MEREDITH: *You know, after losing Robbie I just really became extremely protective and doting and you know, in a sense I had this sense of fear. You lose one child and it affects you, you know, it will affect me for the rest of my life. It just will.*

LYNAE: *Mhm.*

MEREDITH: *It's not something I ever really talked about all that much and that's it and I don't know that I really want to go into it right now, because I'm feeling myself get emotional, and we need to focus on Max. Um, really that's . . . I feel like I've been . . . I know I have been probably over protective, and really doting, and let him get away with things that I probably shouldn't have let, because clearly he's acting out so . . . I hate to admit it but my style of parenting at this point in life is just not working and that's the real reason that I turned to Bill and said "you gotta be the one to take the lead on this, because it's just not my forte right now."*

At that point the room became quiet and awkward. After a few quiet moments Lynae commented about both parents being over protective of Sarah. At that point we realized that Lynae is avoiding the difficult and emotional issue of the loss of Robbie and we pulled her out to discuss what was happening in the session and help her address the issue. We asked her how she felt in the room and what was her sense of what was going on with the clients. She described a strong sense of heaviness, feeling very sad and feeling very lonely, suggesting that the family members felt very lonely in their grief. We asked Lynae to go back into the session and use those feelings to connect with the family and help them feel understood and heard. Lynae goes back into the room to work with the family.

LYNAE: *There are a couple of things that I picked up on. Sarah, you mentioned about that you'd lost a brother you didn't want to lose another one, and Meredith, very sensitive for you, you talked about Max being your baby, and about the loss of Robbie, and everything, I just wanted to know how you Bill, how you feel about that. About Robbie?*

BILL: *I—I mean I was devastated when Robbie died. I mean I was just crushed. Um, and Meredith was more visibly upset about it. I don't know if she was more upset about it though. Me, I felt at the time, cause I still had my little girl you know, who had just lost a brother and she was old enough to understand this stuff and so I put all my energy into her and made sure she's all right. And I felt like, I felt like I took all my pain and I put it in a little pocket.*

Once Lynae was able to connect to her own feelings about the session and engage with the family from that emotional place the tone in the session shifted and they were able to talk about their pain. Below is Lynae's account of what transpired in the session and how she was able to use her *self* to help the clients:

This session triggered my signature theme. I found it very emotional. I knew "intellectually" that Robbie was a key factor and was prepared to raise and address the issue. However as soon as I followed up on Sarah's comment about not wanting "to lose another brother" there was an emotional under current in the room, as if the ice on the surface of the lake had cracked. Each time I went back to Robbie the crack got bigger.

I was completely unprepared for the emotional response from everyone especially myself. When Meredith said she "didn't want to go there" I literally shied away from the topic with relief, because I certainly did not want to go there emotionally. Intellectually was one thing, being there emotionally was another ball game I did not want to play. To do my job which is to help my clients we had to talk about Robbie; giving into my need to shy away would have been a disservice to them and a failure on my part as a therapist. I was like the proverbial rabbit in the headlights; I could not get out of the way. I wanted the clients to tap into their emotions and be vulnerable but I, as the therapist, was not prepared to go into the same place.

Could I really stand on the edge of the lake and assure them that it was ok for them to walk across the ice but not be prepared to demonstrate or step out ahead? Why should they trust me when my words and actions were not congruent? In hindsight I realize that it was quite naïve to think that I could handle something so emotional in an intellectual way; this approach may work in my personal life but it was not my life we were talking about. But then I realized that the clients were doing what I have always done, avoid "going there emotionally," cover up the issue, continue to function but the pain is still there. Avoiding the issue does not work in the long run. At some point if we want to live the best lives we can we have to address the issue head on. All of us in the room, clients and therapist, had to take the risk to trust and be emotionally vulnerable so we could address the issue and make progress.

This was scary ground for me. My instinct would have been to retreat to an "intellectual" place. I went out on a limb and followed Dr. Aponte and Karni's advice to use the emotion I was feeling. Instead of shying away or shutting down, I allowed myself to really feel my emotions. When Bill shared his childhood experience and relived the pain I could truly empathize with him emotionally as opposed to intellectually which I do naturally. I was able to go within myself, tap into memories, cultural beliefs and values yet not be overwhelmed by my own vulnerability and pain. When I reviewed the video of the session I could actually see the difference when the empathy comes from an emotional as opposed to an intellectual place. My voice and tone were softer, my body posture more relaxed. In the session I had felt there was a difference, it was interesting to actually see it on the video. Another lesson I learned was that I went out of my comfort zone because I trusted that Dr. Aponte and Karni would not advise me to do anything that would be harmful or detrimental to my personal well-being. I need to create this same sense of trust and security for my clients.

We use the simlab and the live supervision so we can help trainees connect with their clients in the moment and experience first-hand how using their own brokenness and vulnerability enhances the therapeutic relationship and help the therapy move forward. Lynae was able to challenge herself and go to her dark places in order to connect with her clients. She got to experience how using all of who she is changed the emotional intensity in the room and helped her to empathize with her clients and their pain so that they could directly address their issue.

5 Looking at the POTT Process

The Case of the "Rescuer"

Alba Niño

In this chapter, we will describe in detail the experience of one student who participated in a nine-month POTT class as part of her master's degree program in marriage and family therapy. The student, Darya[1], was a married woman in her early thirties, who had immigrated to the U.S. during her teenage years. The instructors working with this student were Harry Aponte (HJA) and Alba Niño (AN). As described in a previous chapter, the POTT course started with a conceptual introduction of the POTT premises and principles. Then, Darya and her classmates began taking turns presenting to their instructors on their perceptions of their personal core issues, which they introduced through their signature theme papers.

Initial Definition of Signature Themes: Signature Theme Paper

In her initial signature theme paper, Darya related that she is the older of two girls. She and her sister lived with their parents until their parents divorced, when Darya was 11 years old. After living with their maternal grandparents for a few years, Darya and her sister joined their mother and her second husband, who had immigrated to the U.S. In her description of her family history, Darya described several stressors her family faced including substance abuse, mood disorders in both her paternal and maternal sides of the family and certain tragic deaths. These family difficulties, coupled with war, dictatorships and economic instability in her country of origin, contributed to a very stressful childhood.

In her initial paper, Darya identified three preliminary concepts of her signature themes: being unable to ask for help, only connecting with people who have problems and hiding from her own problems. In relation to her understanding of the development of the first signature theme (being unable to ask for help), Darya wrote:

I knew my parents didn't have a happy marriage. Despite their struggles, they kept a calm and friendly atmosphere at home. Therefore, I always felt obligated to protect them as well. I never wanted to add to their already difficult times, so I began hiding my emotions and tried to be as good as possible. As a child, I don't remember ever asking my parents for money, a toy, or anything at all. I never asked for help, I was very independent. If there was something that I couldn't do, or potentially needed my parents' help, I would pretend that I didn't want to do it to begin with, so that I didn't have to trouble my parents.

Darya also found connections between her second signature theme (only connecting with people who have problems) and her family history:

I have developed many coping mechanisms to deal with my family problems of divorce, suicide, immigration, loneliness, depression, addiction and so on, that I feel comfortable and at home with those problems, yet I am extremely uncomfortable around those who to me seem normal and without any problems. As a result, I often find myself in relationships that are emotionally exhausting. My friends usually have problems and always need my help, while I never get a chance to talk about my problems with anyone, and end up just dealing with everything myself.

Finally, Darya explained the relation between her third signature theme (hiding from her own problems) and her family history this way:

I knew my parents had a difficult marriage and there was a lot of sickness in my family. Since we were a close family everyone knew about each other, and everyone's problems were discussed openly. To protect myself form these difficulties, as a defense mechanism, I pretended that everything is fine. I even tried to forget events, such as my aunt and uncle's death or details of my parents' divorce. Today as an adult, I have forgotten many details of my childhood. This is not due to bad memory but a defense mechanism. I don't like to remember anything. So, I believe this a reason for my third signature theme to hide and pretend that everything is OK instead of dealing with issues.

In preparation for Darya's signature theme presentation, we, the instructors, met and discussed how Darya's paper conveyed a great understanding of the *mechanisms* she had developed to *cope* with the difficult situations in her family. We also noted that Darya was not emotionally in touch with the "hurts, disappointments, and losses that form the core of [her] lifelong personal emotional vulnerabilities" (Aponte et al., 2009, p. 384). In other words, she was not emotionally connecting with her signature themes. For that reason, one of our main goals for her signature theme presentation was to help Darya relate emotionally to the more vulnerable aspects of her experience.

Connecting with the Core: Darya's Signature Theme Presentation

As a starting point for the signature theme presentation, one of us (HJA) made a comment meant to highlight for Darya the connections among the three signature themes she had identified in the paper. This comment was also intended to highlight for Darya the contradiction and internal struggle that these coping mechanisms seemed to present for her.

HJA: The first line of the last page says, "I never get a chance to talk about my problems." The last sentence on the last page says, "So, I believe this is the reason for my third signature theme to hide and pretend that everything is OK instead of dealing with issues." On the one hand you say, "I never get a chance to talk about my problems." On the other hand you say, "I don't want to talk about my problems, I just want to avoid them." That seems to sum up the whole paragraph, for me anyway.

DARYA: (giggling) Very interesting. [. . .] I never thought about it that way, I guess. I have always thought that I don't need to talk about anything. [. . .] I guess, as I am getting older my threshold is sort of thinner. As I was saying, all my friends, everybody just always comes to me. And I feel like when I look up, I never, no one really ever asks me. I guess I never looked at it that way, that it's something that bothers me. But now, I'm just looking at my friends and people that I associate with. I feel like I am always there to help them, but I choose people who need help. That is my way of—and I mean I am such a rescuer. I am always a rescuer and I choose those people to go and help them, and naturally they are not the people who are going to rescue me. It's something that I choose, obviously.

HJA: Which is also the way you described your relationship with your parents [citing another quote from her paper]: "I never wanted to add to their overly difficult times so I began hiding my emotions and tried to be as good as possible."

These comments were aimed at highlighting for Darya the way she has pushed away her emotions and needs for the sake of others. Darya seemed to agree with these observations, and she replied with a comment that evinced how, in her relationships, she does not hold others accountable to her. On the contrary, she places most of the responsibility for the relationship on her own shoulders:

DARYA: Yeah, because I feel like—when I was younger it wasn't as much of an issue because you have more energy and you can deal with it. But as things pile up, I feel like I will sit down and say, "What the hell! I need to talk to someone, too. You know?" But I always justify sort of that. Not that it is my fault, but I sort of analyze it and feel like, "Oh yeah, that is my personality, and that is how I choose people." You know what I mean? I never blame it on them, that that's their problem, and that I have a bad friend, but that I choose them because I feel more comfortable with people who have a problem.

In order to help Darya understand the connection between her tendencies to self-sacrifice and justify others, and her deeper relational needs and fears, we offered an example of ways in which children sacrifice themselves for the sake of their parents:

HJA: I will tell you a little story. When I was at [name of institution], they were doing some research and working with children who had physical problems that were closely linked to their emotional state, such as asthma. What they did in the experiment was that they had an observational mirror where you could see the *family but they couldn't see you. And they had the child behind the mirror with a nurse who would periodically take blood samples while the child observed the therapist with the parents. What they would look for was the level of free fatty acids, which indicated levels of stress, and while the therapist on the other side of the mirror would deliberately draw the parents into discussing issues that were potentially conflictual so that the parents would then begin to argue. The overwhelming trend was that these children, as they saw their parents argue, would get their stress levels up. Then, at a certain point, when the stress level was pretty high, the researchers would have the child go into the room with the parents and therapist while the nurse continued to take blood samples. And what the children tended to do was to get in the middle of their parents' fights, and get the parents to start paying attention to them, sometimes even becoming angry with the child. The children would get the parents to stop fighting with each other, and get them to fight with them or simply attend to them. So that when the parents stopped fighting between themselves because they had begun attending to the child, the child's stress level dropped dramatically. It sounded like you (showing the paper to the student).*

DARYA: *Does that sound like me?*

HJA: *Well, (reading from her paper) "I never wanted to add to their already difficult times, so I began hiding my emotions and tried to be as good as possible. I never asked for help." Children will sacrifice themselves in order to prevent their parents from splitting up or argue because that, splitting up, was the most frightening thing. And they would not have their needs met except the need to have their parents together. It sounds like that is what you did with your parents, and then also with friends and everybody in your life. What do you think?*

DARYA: *I am trying to think if that is the problem* [both Darya and we chuckled]. *As I said, I feel like there are times that I feel like I have been so good at act . . . not acting, I don't know, like it becomes part of my personality that I don't know if it is real or I'm still acting or if it's really bothering me or if I'm OK with it. I just I feel like I can't differentiate. That's my defense mechanism, and I feel like it is so strong that I don't differentiate, is it real or is it the defense mechanism?*

With this response, Darya seemed to be moving away from her initial interpretation of her sacrifices to a position where she was questioning herself and her perceptions. We worked to help her start looking at her tendency to hide from her emotional needs as a consequence of the relational patterns and coping mechanisms that she had already identified.

HJA: *The defense mechanism is real.*

DARYA: *But it becomes part of your personality.*

HJA: *Yes, absolutely.*

AN: *What I'm hearing is that it actually makes it hard for you to assess if whatever is happening in front of you bothers you or not, hurts you or not.*

DARYA: *Yes, uhuh.*

AN: *You actually don't know.*

DARYA: *No.*

AN: *Can you give me an example of that?*

DARYA: *Maybe not a specific [example] but maybe—I don't get angry at all just because, maybe with my family, I always justify everything so much. "Okay, this person is going through this problem. Okay, so I shouldn't be angry at them." So, I feel like I don't get angry at all, but there are times that I'm like "If this were another person, they will be angry at something like that." And I don't know if I'm just a chill person—which I don't think I am. I just feel like I justify everything for myself so much that I come to a point that it's just very complicated. Because I feel like I'm not a numb person, I have feelings, but there are certain things that I can't . . . I just justify them so much in my life that now I just can't even get angry. . . . It comes from the fact that I can't react because I feel like throughout my life I have been in situations where I have had to sit down and to justify, justify the situation to make it OK.*

After Darya was able to go from questioning her emotional needs to talking *about* the way she questions her emotions, we found another door to help her connect with the deeper emotions that she had pushed away:

HJA: *Take what you are saying now and put it in the context of how you reacted when your parents were in conflict with each other. What you did with your emotions and judgment of them when they were in conflict with each other, when your intent was for them not to be upset, not to be angry, not to be arguing.*

DARYA: *I wasn't mad at them. Like my dad, he was doing what he was doing. He was doing drugs, whatever. He was a good dad. He was providing for us. It was wrong for him to do that stuff, but I never was really mad at him. My sister was, and she acted out and she had an eating disorder and all that, but I was okay.*

HJA: *You weren't okay.*

DARYA: *Yeah, I wasn't okay.*

HJA: *You suppressed it.*

DARYA: *I was successful* [chuckles, trying to minimize the effects of the comments].

HJA: *You suppressed the anger, which would have separated you from him. And what you did is you allowed in the emotions that were operational, the ones that kept you connected to him. You trained yourself to do that for your mother and father. No matter what they did or how they behaved, you were the one who kept them together and stayed connected. So, you trained yourself from early childhood to suppress your spontaneous reactivity to things that bothered you for people that were most important for you.*

An important part of identifying and defining a signature theme is to help the trainees see how these themes can be important assets in their clinical work. In the next interaction, we see the opportunity to highlight that:

HJA: *Which will make you a great therapist, you see, in the sense that . . .*

DARYA: [inaudible speaking]

HJA: *Well? It's something like that. Why do the people who tell their troubles to the bartender tell their troubles to the bartender? Because the bartender just listens, doesn't get reactive, doesn't judge them and is interested, and so they feel "Oh, I can put it all out there" because they will not get somebody who says* [faking a judgmental tone] *"I can't believe you did that!" And so that invites people to talk and share their problems. In fact, they dump their problems because "this person can handle anything, can hear anything, doesn't judge me, and doesn't get reactive to me." You picked the right profession.*

Our comments, although aiming at showing the ways in which Darya's signature theme can be an asset in her clinical work, also highlighted for her the extent of her self-sacrifice for others. This seemed to help Darya connect with how exhausted she feels about being there for everybody, how hard things have been for her, and especially how abandoned she has felt while taking care of others. Consequently, she shared a poignant episode of her life story:

DARYA: [tears up]

AN: *This is touching something, what's happening?*

DARYA: *I don't know. I feel like at one point it becomes tiresome. Of course, I am not trained to talk, and I hide anyway possible. I seek out the most troubled person and connect with them just because I want them to talk to me, I understand all that. I don't know why. I feel like, not that I want to talk about things, but I feel like I am at the point that I feel like it's a little bit hard for me.*

HJA: *Well you are not getting the love and understanding and the support that you need and you want like anybody else.*

DARYA: *It's just like . . . I will give you an example with my family. When everything was happening with my sister, when she was at the point—I don't even think my mom knows. I never told her, again, because I wanted to always protect her—but my sister was at the point where she couldn't walk anymore because her anorexia was so bad that we had to get her a wheelchair. She couldn't walk. And my mom— because my mom and her had so much conflict between them—my mom decided that she was going to stay out of it. And see if she wanted to go to therapy, and then my mom would stay out of it because my sister would get really upset. So, at one point when my sister was at that stage when she was really bad, my mom decided to go to [country of origin]. Just leave the country and just go. My dad was in [country of origin]. So, it was just me and [Darya's husband's name] taking care of my sister, getting a wheel chair for her, signing her up for rehab and everything. And I did it because it was for my sister, but I feel now, I feel like "why was it just me?" I feel bad for my sister. I feel that everyone, my family, I feel like we are so close and everyone is so lovey-dovey and everyone loves each other. But at the point that everything was going down, it was really crazy, like my sister was dying basically. She was like 2 pounds, she was nothingness. My dad was in [country of origin] and wasn't talking to my sister because he didn't know how to handle it, and my mom ran away. I'm not blaming her because she had a lot of issues that she was dealing with.*

When Darya, as expected, was trying to explain why others were not there for her, an ironic comment by one of us helped her see how she was, yet again, trying to justify others. This comment functioned as a block to her usual defense mechanism, helping her get even more in touch with her vulnerable emotions.

HJA: [ironic tone] *Yes, of course, she had a lot of problems* (Darya and HJA chuckled).

DARYA: *Yeah, but they all ran away. So, it was just me and my sister, and I had no idea what to do. I was in this new relationship with [name of husband] and I was in school, and I had my job, and I could handle it, of course. I did it. She went to rehab and all that, and she came out. But it was just all sort of on me. And at that point I felt like "Enough is enough! Can I take a break here?" and of course, I didn't say anything because I don't know how to say anything. And I think that was the point where I just started getting tired after that.*

Darya had expressed the unfairness and the exhaustion of having to take care of others in her family. And she did it by describing how she was left alone in what was perhaps the scariest moment of her life: seeing her sister emaciated by a life-threatening eating disorder. After this, we presented Darya with a hypothesis of what could be behind her tendency to justify others and avoid asking for help.

HJA: *I wonder whether you live with the question "Is the person on the other side of me, will that person want to hear my thoughts? Does that person want to bear the burden of my problems? I'm not accustomed to having people who I can trust completely that they will listen to me and take on my problems the way I'm wanting to listen to them and take on their problems."*

DARYA: *But I guess that is just . . . I can't trust. I don't look at my mom and dad as adults. They're adults. They're 50 or 60 years or whatever, and they are adults for their friends. My mom has people calling her for advice. She is an amazing woman. But for me, I can't rely on her. I don't look at my parents as adults, and I always look at it as I am their parent, sort of. But, I don't know, that is my problem. If I tell my mom, she will be like "what the hell are you talking about?" But that's how I feel and that's why I can't go to her . . .*

HJA: *Yeah, you are saying a lot with that. Because what you are saying is that, "I have been conditioned to expect that if I am going to have an intimate relationship with someone, with somebody that I really care about, I can't trust that that person will want to remain with me if I open up with that person all of my problems, all of my insecurities, all of my fears, all of my needs, that that person will really want to listen to that with the readiness to be there for me, to bear the burden of me just because they love me."*

DARYA: *Are you saying that I have a fear of losing people? Because I don't think I do.*

HJA: *Well, I don't know if your parents would have been there for you, if you had dumped all your problems on them when they were having all their problems. Your mother ran away. She ran away to [country of origin] when your sister was having her problems. The message you got from both your parents was that when things got really bad with their children they couldn't handle it.*

DARYA: *But I don't have a fear of losing them because I feel that I am so self-reliant that I feel like "OK."*

Borrowing from systemic theory, attachment theory and humanistic perspectives, as POTT instructors we ascribe to a view of human beings as social beings, who need love, connections, support and communication with other human beings to feel safe, form a sense of self, be healthy and thrive. This essential definition of the human condition aids us in challenging Darya's perception of her self-reliance.

HJA: *You have so conditioned yourself that you have virtually killed the awareness of your need and desire to have somebody hold you when you are ready to fall. It's so automatic that you don't even recognize that you, like everybody else, want to live with the assurance that "if I start to fall, really fall, that the person who loves me is going to want to hold me, and stay with me, and stop me from falling down no matter how long it will take, no matter how heavy I am at that moment with my problem." It's like you don't know that.*

DARYA: *My question is, "Does that exist? Do people think that there is someone like that in their lives?"* [Darya chuckles]

HJA: *I can assure you, you will be that kind of parent with your child.*

DARYA: *Yeah, and I was like that with my sister, I guess.*

HJA: *And you will be that. You will be that way even much more with your child and your child will know it, and your child will have that assurance.*

DARYA: *That's true.*

In addition to helping students connect with the vulnerable emotions that are at the core of their signature themes, we also help them get a better idea of the effects of their signature themes on their relationships. This awareness, of course, will later on assist students in understanding how their signature themes will play out in their therapeutic relationships.

AN: *One of the things that you mentioned in the paper was that you see this "not asking for help and not disclosing," that this actually gets in the way of your relationship with your husband.*

DARYA: *Yeah, because I don't know how to ask for help; even the smallest thing. If the water is boiling and it's coming up, and I'm doing something else and he's standing there, I can't ask him to go over and turn the stove down. I have to jump and do it, and stuff like that. It's so minute but it piles up because I never ask for help, never.*

HJA: *You know what he is experiencing? "You don't let me love you."*

DARYA: *Yeah, and he gets frustrated because he feels that I don't trust him and it's just . . .*

HJA: *That "I don't trust him to love me so much that he would want to go out of his way to inconvenience himself, even risk himself, in order to take care of me." [. . .]*

And so what that does in your relationship with your husband is it creates a certain distance, an emotional distance, because he can't get as close to you as he wants to be. And getting close to you doesn't mean you are giving to him. He wants to be able to give to you.

AN: How are you doing now?

DARYA: *(tearing up)* I think it upsets me more when thinking about my relationship with [husband's name] because I feel like he wants to do anything that he can. [. . .] I don't allow him to do anything for me, and if that would become a problem between us, that would be horrifying to me, more than anything else.

HJA: And that will become more of an issue when you have a child because he will want to be there for you and for the child, not just for the child, but for you and the child. And you are going to need support. You are going to need partnership. This is the way of loving. He needs to be able to give his love to someone who wants and needs his love, and if he doesn't feel needed it makes his love unimportant.

DARYA: *(tearing up)* Yeah, that bothers me and I feel like I don't give him a chance, and I am aware of it. I don't ask for anything and it bothers me, not because . . . I don't know how to explain it. It's really complicated for me. Even the little things, I take the trash out, and I do the dishes, I do everything and they are not important, I know, and when I see him I feel like this guy is standing there wanting to do things for me. He wants to. I do everything. I feel like I am a control freak. I do grocery shopping. If he tells me he wants to go grocery shopping, I'm like "no, no, no I'll do it."

By exploring the impact of her signature theme in her personal relationships, we also help Darya expand the meaning of giving and receiving in relationships. This is especially important when considering the therapeutic relationship. Being able to give, receive and partner with clients will help trainees work *with* their clients, rather than just do things *for* their clients.

HJA: He wants to be able to love you, and to love you means that he wants to be able to be there for you. He wants to be able to partner with you. He wants to be able to make your life a little easier. He wants to feel needed by you so that he can give to you, which is a way of loving you. And because of the relationship you have with your parents, and the training and the conditioning, it doesn't come naturally to you. So the control freak thing is part of what you needed to do to be able to suppress your need for your parents to be there for you.

When helping trainees connect with their own humanity, and understand their own human struggles, it is always important to validate their coping mechanisms, and stress the importance of these mechanisms for their survival. Understanding and validating coping and defense mechanisms in their own lives helps trainees extend this validation and understanding to their clients.

AN: If you had not done that, if you had not taken charge in your own family, what would have happened? You didn't have two adults as parents.

DARYA: *Probably what happened with my sister; because right now my mom and dad call me every day. They don't call my sister, and she is the one who is alone, and she has problems and they just don't; not because they don't love her, they just don't know how to handle it. If I had problems, maybe they wouldn't listen to me, you know?*

AN: *So you had to take over. So you had to take control. And my impression is that it is really hard to feel that somebody else can be there. And that if you are not in control, yes, that is scary because that was scary at some point. You had to take control, you had to step up and figure out how to handle a father that didn't know what to do and a mother that would freak out and a sister that was reacting to all that. And so, you figured it out. And now you don't want to get rid of that. You learned something and "I want to continue to use it no matter what," but that strategy that you learned can hurt your relationships.*

DARYA: *Um-hmm.*

HJA: *And you are going to see that in your cases. That to receive love is not as easy as it sounds because to receive love and ask for love, to need the love, to communicate the need for the love means that you become vulnerable and risk being disappointed.*

AN: *And give up control a little bit.*

HJA: *A lot, a lot.*

After a few more closing comments, the forum was open for the rest of the students to share with Darya how her story resonated with and affected them. This concluded the signature theme presentation. In the paper following her signature theme presentation, Darya described a deeper understanding of her signature theme. The following excerpts of her paper show how Darya was not only aware of her coping mechanism, but had also connected with her fears of being burdensome and of abandonment, and her longing to have more balanced relationships where she is also loved and cared for. She is even able to see that her friends not only need her, but also would like to be there for her (emphasis added).

I am starting to recognize my signature themes' effects on daily interactions and decisions. Inconveniencing others is almost a phobia for me. However my definition of burden and inconvenience, influenced by my defense mechanisms and signature themes, is an out of proportion monster of a definition. To me, if I am not absolutely needed, if I am not helping and affecting someone's life in a meaningful and positive way, if I am not making a positive change or doing something "meaningful," I should stay out of sight, fearing that I am burdening people. This has often offended my friends, co-workers and family, who think I am only around if there is a problem.

Although I didn't think of this as my signature theme, in POTT, I learned that I am afraid of abandonment. I am always there for others and never bother them with my problems because I am scared that they will reject me. My family always struggled with some problems. [. . .] However, no one really was good at addressing these issues and solving problems. Instead, they always left the person in trouble to deal with issues alone. Emotionally everyone felt extremely saddened by these situations and felt incapable to help. Subconsciously as a child, I learned to act strong or I would be left alone as well. After our discussions in POTT, I realized that I always had a subconscious fear of being left alone, so I created a complex defense mechanism to protect myself. By suppressing my emotional needs I was not bothering people with my problems, so they could continue with their lives without any concerns about me, and by being a selfless friend, or family member I was always there for others to stop them from abandoning me.

Working Clinically with the Signature Theme: Simlab

After trainees have a better understanding of their signature themes and are more at ease with connecting with the hurts, needs and vulnerable emotions that lie at their core, the training shifts its emphasis to helping trainees to more consciously and purposefully use themselves and their personal issues in their clinical work. This is the main purpose of activities such as the simlab experience and the case presentation.

In her signature theme paper, Darya had already identified how her difficulty asking for help and her tendency to protect and rescue others could potentially jeopardize her clinical work:

I believe that for therapy to be effective it must be a work between the patient and the therapist. I am afraid that at times I will do the work for my patients and not allow them to go through the process that they need to go through to get the results they are asking for. I also need to consider consulting with my supervisors and peers in issues that are not clear to me. I am afraid if I don't recognize my hang-ups and live unaware to my signature theme, this will stop me from seeking help and supervision. Also, if I am inexpert to ask for help, and unable to open myself up to others, this would be a contradiction to my practice of asking my patients to open up and ask for help.

Through the simlab[2], Darya became aware of the salient relational implications of her signature themes in her clinical work. The "clients" in the simlab experience were a heterosexual married couple drifting apart after facing several problems, including the husband's unemployment and depression, and the suspicion that the wife had been unfaithful. In this case, the female client was more vocal and assertive, and the man was less able to speak up to get his point across. Darya found herself losing her capacity to connect with both partners at the same time, and ended up allying with the person she perceived as weaker and, therefore, more in need of being rescued and protected:

On the surface my clients presented me with two completely different personalities. The wife seemed emotionally resilient and independent while the husband seemed more sensitive and hurt. Based on my signature theme, as a rescuer, I was automatically drawn to the husband (the person who initially seemed more hurt to me). Since the wife had a persona of a person who may not need help in handling hardships in life, initially I dismissed her feelings, assuming that she is able to handle herself and her problems well, and not in need of my help.

Although it is important for trainees to raise their awareness about the ways in which their signature themes can hamper their clinical work, the main purpose of POTT is not to act as a cautionary tale to keep trainees vigilant about making a mistake. On the contrary, POTT's main goal is to help trainees connect with their own humanity and woundedness as a source of compassion for and understanding of their clients. Darya was very keen about noticing how her signature theme made her prone to connect with those that she perceived as less powerful in a family or a couple. However, she also learned that understanding her fears and struggles, and the way she manages them in relationships (e.g. hiding her vulnerability, helping others rather than putting herself in the position of asking for help) could be an extraordinary source of wisdom about the human experience. In fact, it was Darya's understanding of her own process that helped her reach a different view of the wife and her experience:

However, after listening to them more carefully, I was able to see that the wife was equally hurt in her marriage, and also was similar to her husband in her need for connection and love from her spouse. I started to recognize her as someone similar to myself. Someone who may need help, but is unable to ask for it. In my opinion she was hiding her emotions behind a shield of pseudo strength and defensiveness (as part of my signature theme, in order to survive hardships by myself, I needed to develop an independent personality and remain self-reliant throughout my life). As I became more aware of the wife's underlying struggles regarding her relationship with her husband, I started to connect with her based on my personal similarities with her, and from there I could balance my attention and connection to them more equally.

In her simlab experience, Darya was also able to experience in action how her tendency to rescue can affect the type of interaction that she establishes with her clients:

As a rescuer I jump to help others, sometimes without them even asking. In the session with my clients I became aware of how strong this subconscious force influences my relationships and interactions. Initially in the session I was not even allowing my clients to talk and fully unfold themselves for me. I realized that I was not even listening to them and was so pre-occupied to find a solution for their problems right away. At this point, I was becoming frustrated and self-conscious (based on my signature theme I see my worth only when I can be "useful" and helpful to others) therefore in my mind I had to have an answer for my clients right away to help them and to satisfy myself.

The greatest advantage of the simlab experience is for the students to be able to receive feedback from the instructors as the mock therapy session is happening. This allows the students to change their approach with their clients. As students incorporate in their sessions the feedback provided by the instructors, they get to experience themselves differently in relation to their clients. During her simlab, we asked Darya to step out of the therapy room momentarily, so we could share our observations and provide specific recommendations.

After receiving instructions from Dr. Aponte and Alba, I tried to allow my clients to go through the process and naturally come to their own conclusions and answers by recognizing their own struggles and strengths. At this point I was more relaxed and connected to my clients and the session was more productive for my clients and myself alike. I also could feel that as I was allowing them to go through the process more organically the tension between them was lessening and they were starting to connect to each other more.

Working Clinically with the Signature Theme: Case Presentation

In her simlab experience, Darya was able to see in action her tendency to ally with and rescue the person she perceived as weaker or less powerful. Reaching this clarity about her own process allowed her to see that this tendency was also affecting her clinical work at the school where she was placed for her practicum:

Often I find myself deeply connected with the children but disconnected from their parents or teacher who initially have referred them to me for certain problems they have been trying to work on. I find myself connecting with those who are in need of help without taking into consideration the feelings of the more strong person in the relationship [. . .] I never considered myself as an unfair person. However, I am afraid if I don't address this issue correctly it will affect my clients negatively, in thinking that I may be treating each person differently based on their strength in the relationship. This is an interesting manifestation of my signature theme.

For her case presentation, Darya brought up the case of Nick[3], a 16-year-old White adolescent male who self-referred for therapy to deal with his "anger issues." Divorce, substance abuse, imprisonment, placement in foster homes and death in his family kept him from having a nurturing, dependable and consistent parental figure in his life. After several years of separation due to incarceration, Nick's father, Henry, was the person now taking care of him. In his sessions, Nick disclosed that he was a gang member, and described for Darya many of their activities and crimes. His chaotic life awakened Darya's interest and her proneness to rescuing:

I immediately was drawn to his life and his stories because his upbringing and his family dynamics were very foreign to me. I also have found a perfect client in Nick, for me to protect and nurture. [. . .] I was very protective of him and his emotions and very judgmental of his parents. When I first met his father, I was ready to attack him, and was very judgmental of his parenting style. This judgment prevented me from investigating to see whether there is any love or emotional connection in the family regardless of its chaos and dramas. I also became very protective of him [Nick]. To this day, my nurturer part would not allow me to challenge him enough to work harder, for example in expressing emotions other than anger.

Darya had a hard time finding ways to be helpful to Nick, and that was the main reason she wanted to bring this case to the POTT class in her case presentation. Even though Darya could understand Nick's reality beyond his anger and his gang involvement, she still had a difficult time feeling that she could connect with his experience given the vast differences in their worlds.

At times I am very lost with him because I feel there is nothing that I can help him with. [. . .] My biggest challenge is to truly believe that I can have a positive impact on his life. [. . .] In my opinion, Nick feels the burden of growing up without a guide on his shoulders and is frightened. His father is there, but Nick doesn't see him as one who can help him in life. Therefore, he engages in gang activities in order to fill that void and to gain a pseudo sense of strength and security. [. . .] I believe my main challenge with Nick is our extremely different life experiences and upbringing. This world of gangs, violence, prison system and life in the streets is very foreign to me. My curiosity of learning about his life has helped us to create a trusting therapeutic relationship. Yet, in my opinion, it has prevented me from getting past the extravaganza of his stories in order to reach the underlying problems such as fears, insecurities and sense of abandonment.

During her presentation, it became evident to us that, despite many contextual differences (gender, age, country of origin, socioeconomic status, etc.) there were remarkable experiential commonalities between Nick's current situation and Darya's upbringing. The two of them had to figure out how to navigate a chaotic and frightening world without having the support and guidance of a dependable parent. The two of them had to develop ways to suppress their vulnerable emotions and disconnect from their basic emotional needs in order to survive. Therefore, during the case presentation, we pointed out to Darya that she had more in common with Nick than she was allowing herself to see, and that it was at this human level that she could find a genuine connection with Nick. Darya was invited to connect with her own fears of being abandoned, and with her own frustration for not having a parent to lean on, and through these experiences, connect with Nick at an emotional level. Darya was encouraged to use her own experience to intuit how Nick could be feeling, and to communicate this deeper understanding of his experience to him. Using her experience to connect to Nick's experience radically changed the way Darya saw Nick as a person, as reported in the paper that followed her case presentation:

Due to my parents' chaotic lives when I was growing up, my childhood was filled with fears and insecurities. I felt that I had no one to rely on and had to protect myself. That was awfully scary. Nick's parents also have their own chaotic lives, dealing with child [protective] services and prisons, drug addiction, unemployment and so on. Nick is left to rely on nobody but himself. He needs to be serious and resilient in order to survive; yet he is only a child, and the responsibility of being on his own is terrifying him. By realizing this similarity between Nick and myself now I can see beyond our artificial differences and get close to the similar emotional experiences I had as a child, which brings me closer to understanding him and further helping him. I believe before my POTT session I acted more as a voyeur looking into his life from an outside world, trying to learn and make sense of it. In every session I sat across from him and observed him as a gang member, as a child without a family, as the son of a prostitute, etc., yet I never thought about these facts as artificial barriers, which stopped me from truly understanding him as a suffering child, very similar to myself at his age.

Darya also reached a different understanding of the effects of her protective tendencies and coping mechanisms in the therapeutic process with Nick.

To this day my nurturer part would not allow me to challenge him enough to work harder, for example in expressing emotions other than anger. I have allowed him to open up, to share the most disturbing experiences he has with gang violence and other activities he engages in, yet my challenge as a therapist is to take him further to get deeper to his insecurities, fears and loneliness. I now understand that since my defense mechanism against getting emotionally hurt is to forget the past by blocking it from my memory and never acknowledging the occurrence of the hurtful incidences, I was protecting Nick similarly by not challenging him enough to get deeper into his emotions and sufferings. I now understand that I was protective of Nick because I didn't want to see his vulnerable side. Since I hide behind my defense mechanisms to protect myself, I was not ready to see Nick truly open up either; therefore I failed to challenge him to get to that deeper, vulnerable place.

The POTT training aims to enhance therapeutic effectiveness of trainees by helping them purposefully use who they are in their clinical work. However, the disciplined and arduous work of making one's own experience more accessible to oneself in order to use it in the work with clients also lends to personal transformations. Thus, in the final writing of the case, important parts of Darya's experience that she had pushed away from her memory were coming back to be part of her full narrative. Through a process of self-exploration and validation, her emotions and needs started to reclaim their place in Darya's life story.

Growing up, I never got a sense that I could trust any of the adults. I learned early on not to rely on anyone for help and support. As a result I had a very anxious childhood filled with migraine headaches, suppressed anger and fear. Although our fears manifest in different ways, in realizing my similarities with Nick, I feel much closer to him and much better able to help him. I can remember my reactions and anxiety when as a child I felt lonely. Not lonely in a sense that there was no one to play with or my parents were not there physically, but a different type of loneliness where I thought and felt I was on my own if anything bad happened since everyone was so involved in their own dramas and problems. I was afraid to go to school because the school environment was too out of my control, I preferred to stay home where I had a bit more control, therefore miraculously I would get migraine headaches a few times a week to keep me out of school very similar to Nick who has a rich history of injuries which have kept him from coming to school for long periods of time (and I believe from gang involvement as well).

After her case presentation, Darya not only had a much better connection with her client, but also a better sense that she could be helpful to him. She also had a clearer understanding of how to use her own life experience in her clinical work.

This process was unbelievably interesting to me because I believe I started to understand the core of what we try to do and the connections that we need to make with our clients. It is easy to be distracted by the superficial differences we each have with our clients. I now believe I am starting to understand once these barriers are crossed, even the client who is poles apart from me perhaps at one point had experienced similar fears, disappointments and anxieties as mine. This understanding now allows me to be sympathetic with my clients, not merely with compassion and kindness but with strong feelings that are rooted in my own experiences.

Weekly Journals

Weekly journals in the POTT class provide students with the opportunity to regularly reflect on their own process. The journals provide continuity in the POTT process, and maintain students' engagement even when they are not in the spotlight, but are witnesses of their classmates' journeys. Journals are the space for students to distill the lessons learned in every class session when they listen to their classmates' stories or see them in their clinical work. Darya, for example, was able to reach a deeper understanding of her tendency to push away memories after watching a classmate's signature theme presentation. In one of her journals, Darya reported:

I was very affected by [name of classmate]'s presentation. It made me realize the value of looking back into our hardships and difficulties and use them as therapeutic tools to connect and help our clients. I always try to forget the past and never re-visit my hard memories. However more and more I am realizing those memories are part of what would help me to get connected to my clients and understand them better in order to help them.

Watching classmates in the role of therapist is also a learning experience for students in POTT. This provides students with contrasting approaches to therapy, and different interventions. In Darya's case, she learned about the value of not "jumping into problem solving" by watching a classmate with a very different therapeutic style. This classmate was seeing the same case that Darya had seen in her simlab. The wife was unable to attend this particular session, so the classmate conducted an individual session with the husband. The following are Darya's impressions about her classmate's simlab as reported in her weekly journal:

In today's Sim Lab and how [classmate's name] was conducting the therapy I realized that I was getting very frustrated. I was ready to give him [the client] solutions right away and could not understand [classmate]'s approach. After watching the feedback session I realized how [classmate]'s style and attitude helped him [client] to open up to her and was able to connect and trust her. He said it was helpful to him to just vent especially in this session that his wife was absent; he got a chance to talk about what he normally would not be able to speak about in her presence.

POTT is a journey that combines the intense experience of presentations and simulated sessions, with the constant reflecting on the experience in the form of papers and journals. It is through this combination of experience and reflection that students get a better understanding of their own emotional and relational processes. It is through this duality that students become better able to access the richness of their own lived experience and connect their client's humanity. It is through this experiential and reflective process that they become more present for their clients in the therapy room.

Notes

1 Names and other identifying information have been changed or purposefully left vague to protect the identity of this trainee.
2 Usually, case presentations happen before the simlabs. However, for this particular cohort, the simlabs occurred first. This way, the students had more time to work with clients in their clinical placements that they can discuss in their case presentation.
3 The names of the client and his family members have been changed to protect their identities.

Reference

Aponte, H.J., Powell, F.D., Brooks, S., Watson, M.F., Litzke, C. Lawless, J. & Johnson, E. (2009). Training the person of the therapist in an academic setting. *Journal of Marital and Family Therapy*, *35*, 381–394.

6 About the Facilitators

Karni Kissil

In this chapter we will cover the implementation of the POTT model focusing on the facilitators. We will describe how the facilitators are trained, the basic requirements and qualifications of the facilitators and what exactly the facilitators do to make the POTT model effective and safe for the trainees.

Facilitator Training

In order to become a POTT facilitator you have to be an active therapist (any discipline). Being an approved supervisor in your discipline is preferable, or having some supervisory experience or training to become a supervisor. Although the POTT training program is not therapy, POTT facilitators use their clinical skills and experience when working with trainees. They are helping students uncover, explore and conceptualize core emotional issues of theirs, along with recognizing the ways these issues affect their thinking and functioning, and finally how to take responsibility for working with and through these issues in their interactions with clients. Therefore, they have to be comfortable and familiar engaging in clinical interactions. POTT facilitators have to be skilled at connecting to their trainees enough to be able to identify with their struggles and pain while at the same time stay differentiated enough that they can help the trainees use their woundedness without getting lost in it. POTT facilitators have to be able to hold the intensity of the interaction with the trainee while being mindful of the other trainees present so this trainee and all the others who are watching the interaction feel safe knowing that the trainers are competent and able to deal with every experience they bring up and that they are safe being vulnerable in class.

Additionally, POTT facilitators have to gain first-hand experience of the POTT training. To be comfortable helping the trainees and providing a safe holding environment for them, facilitators have to know what it feels like to participate in the training, and have to be able to feel comfortable with their own woundedness and humanity. By walking through the same steps the trainees are required to walk through, the facilitators can more easily empathize with the trainees' experiences in the training and be powerful role models. In addition, by going through the training themselves facilitators get a clearer understanding of the fine line the POTT training walks between training and therapy. While the training can feel therapeutic at times, POTT facilitators learn how to maintain the boundaries so it does not become therapy. The focus is always—in class discussions, presentations, write-ups and journals—on how to use the self for the benefit *of the clients* and how trainees can apply what they learn to their clinical work.

The training of the facilitators includes several steps:

1. Reading available publications about the POTT training. The reading materials include the following articles:

- Aponte, H.J. (1994b). How personal can training get? *Journal of Marital and Family Therapy, 20*(1), 3–15.
  [This article discusses the fine line between training and therapy, and explains how the POTT model allows for training with therapeutic *qualities* while maintaining clear professional boundaries to make sure the training does not become therapy.]
- Aponte, H.J. & Carlsen, J.C. (2009). An instrument for the person-of-the-therapist supervision. *Journal of Marital and Family Therapy, 35*, 395–405.
  [This article discusses the use of a specific instrument for taking into account the POTT when presenting cases, and provides case presentations to illustrate how to use the instrument in supervision within this supervisory model.]
- Aponte, H. & Kissil, K. (2012). "If I can grapple with this I can truly be of use in the therapy room": Using the therapist's own emotional struggles to facilitate effective therapy. *Journal of Marital and Family Therapy*. DOI: 10.1111/jmft.12011.
  [This article discusses the concept of the signature theme and demonstrates, step-by-step, how we work with our trainees in the training program, to teach them how to become aware, accept and effectively use their signature themes in their clinical work.]
- Aponte, H.J., Powell, F.D., Brooks, S., Watson, M.F., Litzke, C. Lawless, J. & Johnson, E. (2009). Training the person of the therapist in an academic setting. *Journal of Marital and Family Therapy, 35*, 381–394.
  [This article discusses the POTT model and describes its first time implementation in an accredited MFT graduate program.]
- Lutz, L. & Irizarry, S.S. (2009). Reflections of two trainees: Person-of-the-therapist training for marriage and family therapists. *Journal of Marital and Family Therapy, 35*, 370–380.
  [This last article describes the experiences of two trainees who went through the POTT training in an MFT graduate program.]

Experiential component: The facilitators are expected to undergo the POTT training experience where, ideally, they get a chance to present to an experienced POTT facilitator on their own signature theme at least twice, and three times on self vis-à-vis clinical cases. It will be to the advantage of the facilitator in training to undergo the training with at least one other trainee to have the experience of a peer participating who can offer feedback and support, and to whom he/she can also offer feedback and support, simulating the group experience of the students. As we discussed in Chapter 2, our experience taught us that the group amplifies the power of the experience exponentially. The group allows the individual trainee to see the humanity of every other trainee, who like their clients and themselves, struggles with life. It helps remove the shame that blinds us to our flaws and vulnerabilities, provides the support of empathic colleagues and facilitates the ability to observe self by seeing ourselves as others see us. Facilitators who go through the training in a group format are better able to later empathize with their trainees, having experienced themselves the intensity of the process. It also makes it easier for the facilitator to help trainees transfer what they learned about understanding and empathizing with another person's woundedness (from their experiences relating to their presenting classmates) to the way they relate to their clients.

Similar to the process trainees go through, the facilitator trainees are instructed to provide feedback to their presenting peers addressing how what they experienced in the presentation resonated with them; their signature theme/s, life experiences, thoughts and feelings about themselves. We found this way of providing feedback crucial to maintaining a sense of safe holding environment which is so important for this work.

2. Presenting on the signature theme: Facilitators use the same instrument used in the POTT training to become familiar with their signature theme. POTT facilitators present their signature theme so that they may know what a signature theme is from their own experience. It is a difficult concept to understand in depth, and wrestling with it yourself helps the facilitator to grasp how powerful it is while also how complex in all of its transformations and manifestations. Typically, the facilitator will prepare the signature theme paper at home and will send it ahead of time to the trainer and fellow facilitator trainees. The process is similar to the one the trainees go through described in Chapter 2.

3. Presenting clinical/supervision cases. Ideally, facilitators have three case presentations. The first presentation on a case would be the presentation of a video where the facilitators in training are helped to identify how their signature theme/s affected the three aspects of the therapeutic process—the relationship, assessment and intervention. The second case presentation would focus on how the facilitator attempted to use self purposefully and actively in a therapy session. The third presentation would be a live supervisory experience where the trainer can guide the facilitator trainee in the active and purposeful use of self with a client family. Facilitator trainees use the same instrument that trainees use to write-up their cases. They can present cases involving clients or supervisees. This part of the training is crucial because this is the essence and the ultimate goal of the POTT training: help trainees make the connection between their signature themes and their clinical work so they can use the former to improve the latter. Going through this part of the training helps facilitators learn and experience how to make this connection and use what they learned about themselves to better connect, assess and intervene with their clients, supervisees or students.

Following the training, facilitators should continue to work at least for another year on refining and distilling their understanding of their signature themes and their manifestations in their clinical work. They can do so by apprenticing with someone who is trained in the POTT model, and/or by being supervised while facilitating a POTT training program.

On Being a Co-Facilitator

A co-facilitator team within the POTT model calls for complementarity and congruence to achieve an effective collaboration at both personal and professional levels. Because of the complexity of the human experience— emotional, social and spiritual—it is to the advantage of the facilitators to bring a broad range of personal experience to the encounter with a trainee. The range of personal experience should allow for greater potential for personal identification and differentiation on the parts of the facilitators, which promote both greater resonance and objectivity in the evolving therapeutic process. A variety of professional experience and orientation between the two facilitators also helps ensure that they make room for trainees to present their clinical work from perspectives that fit who they are, and need not conform to the therapeutic orientations of the POTT facilitators, who should be encouraging individuation on the part of the trainees.

For the POTT facilitators *congruence* means more "harmony" than "agreement." The implication is that the dynamics of identification and differentiation should also operate between them both personally and professionally. The facilitators should be in places in their own personal and professional development that they can interweave their respective personal issues and vulnerabilities, as well as their personal experiences and professional orientations with a facility and adeptness that makes for a particularly enriching and freeing encounter for the trainee. Congruence here speaks to where the individual facilitators have grown in their own knowledge of self, acceptance of self and freedom with self that they can engage in the intricacies of the disciplined freedom of the work with the trainee and each other with ever more of who they are both personally and professionally.

The Work of the Facilitators

This section of the manual describes how we, the facilitators of the POTT training, make it work. We will break the process down into small parts by answering questions we are often asked when we present on the training.

1. How do we as facilitators make the training safe?

Acknowledging the emotionally challenging nature of this training, we work continuously to create a safe holding environment by putting in place solid structure and guidelines for the training process, clear group rules regarding confidentiality and feedback providing, and by facilitating a non-judgmental and accepting training environment. We are always clearly in control of the process in the way we form a relationship with the group, by keeping everyone in the group within boundaries and by actively and purposefully following the stated goals of the training with each trainee. By demonstrating our professional authority over the process the trainees understand and trust the purpose of what we ask of them and our ability to get them there safely. This way they experience their public self-disclosure and self-examination as something that leads to their better understanding of themselves, and to increased mastery of themselves in the use of themselves with all of their flaws in the service of more effective therapy. In addition, throughout the training trainees are instructed to present only as much as they feel comfortable sharing given that the emphasis is more on their reactions to their life experiences than the details of these experiences. The trainers clarify from the start that POTT is not therapy. The focus is always—in class discussions, presentations, write-ups and journals—on how to use the self for the benefit of the clients and how they can apply what they learn to their clinical work.

2. How do we make the students comfortable and willing to be open and vulnerable?

From the very start of the training we convey our strong belief in our shared humanity; we are all flawed, we all struggle. We normalize our vulnerability as a universal condition. We share our underlying philosophy about our flaws and vulnerabilities being opportunities necessary for growth and change. Then we take it one step forward and state clearly that because of these flaws and struggles we can be better therapists. Our flaws can be assets to us in our clinical work because through them we can connect, assess and intervene more effectively with our clients. We demonstrate this thinking to our students throughout our work with them when they share their vulnerabilities and receive our firm validation of their struggles and our guidance in understanding how to channel those unwanted/shameful parts into effective clinical work.

Throughout the training, we emphasize to the trainees that they are free to share as much as they are comfortable sharing. There is no pressure to divulge any details of their life experiences since our focus is on their emotional reactions to their life stories and not the details themselves. As the training progresses and trainees experience our supportive reactions toward them and their classmates, they become more comfortable with their own experiences and more comfortable being vulnerable in the group. Further, our trainees usually emphasize that hearing other trainees' feedback about being able to relate to their experiences creates a sense of being understood and not being alone, which promotes a greater level of comfort about having "issues."

3. How do we help trainees clarify their signature themes? How do we know based on one paper what the signature theme is?

It is much like what we need to learn to do in therapy when we are trying to identify the underlying core dynamic behind the issue the client presents. Again, the POTT process touches on all the elements of the therapeutic process—trust in the relationship, assessing and understanding key issues with their underlying core dynamics, and finally helping people get to a place where their issues are no longer driving their lives because they are reclaiming control over their lives. We are looking for repetition of a relational pattern that can help explain what hinders the trainee's freedom. We look to a story that will tie together the trainee's personal history with the way he/she relates to self and others. We look for the major force that drives and shapes the trainee's relationships; for example, a trainee that because of her chaotic childhood always needs to be in control and not need anyone. As a result she never reaches out to others when she struggles and ends up feeling anxious and unloved behind her projection of a super-competent professional.

After we read and discuss the trainees' signature theme papers we have a clearer idea of what the signature theme might be. During the trainees' presentations we work together to build a coherent story that will bring together their personal history, their ongoing struggle with this specific issue and how they experience it manifesting in different areas of their lives. Then, and most importantly, we take it a step forward to their clinical work and help the trainees understand how this ongoing struggle can help them relate and work with their clients and their struggles.

4. What happens if we think the trainee has a different signature theme than the one he/she presents?

Sometimes a trainee we work with seems not ready to get deep into the core issue. We always validate the normalcy of their experiences. We do not want the trainee to become defensive and shut down. We want them to know that whatever they feel in the moment of their encounter with us makes sense. Through their positive interaction with us they become less guarded and more willing to engage in an honest interaction with us and reflect on our feedback.

When we realize that our understanding of the trainee's issue and the trainee's presented issue are different, we first look for a bridge to connect the two. Sometimes we see different layers of the same theme (for example, a need to be in control and underneath it fear of abandonment). We also look to see whether what they present as their theme offers a path to what we believe is closer to their core issue. In their narrative about their issue and its history we will find some thread that will lead us closer to the core of their issue.

We never force an interpretation. There will be other opportunities to touch on what we believe to be closer to the core force. We may even be able to address it through someone else's presentation that without alluding to the trainee in question, who is not presenting, gives us the opportunity to speak about the issue of the one presenting in a way that we believe may resonate with the person not presenting. In the end we will never impose an interpretation, and will go only as far as we can with any particular individual, hoping that their process of self-exploration will be ongoing, throughout their professional career.

It is important to let the trainees name their own theme. We know that each theme has layers and different aspects to it. The same title can mean different things to different trainees, and the way they make sense of it is idiosyncratic to their history and experiences. When the trainees *own* their themes and create a coherent story that explains how it came to be, they are in a better place to accept it and then use it in their work which is the ultimate goal of this process.

5. What do we look for in the trainees' case presentations?

We are looking for the connections between the trainees' personal issues, history and life experience and the clients themselves with their issues, history and life experiences. We look to free the trainees to dig deeply and instinctively for connections that may be hidden in differences between their own and their clients' experiences that enable the trainees to bridge relational gaps between themselves and their clients. In particular, the focus is on how each trainee's personal life experiences help the trainee relate effectively to the client, understand the client's issue and discover ways to be of help to the client (individual, couple or family). The challenge we often have to deal with is helping the trainees to shift their perspective from experiencing their issues as hindering therapy to seeing how they can effectively use them to improve their work.

6. How can we expect the students to be vulnerable with us and their classmates and then at the end of the hour just pick up and go?

We work with our students as we do with clients (another learning experience for trainees) by pacing the presentation so that by the end of the presentation we have hopefully helped the trainee feel that she/he has gained and accomplished something in *this* particular presentation. We try to make sure that by the end of the presentation the trainees have a better understanding of their theme and a clearer direction for the steps they need to take in their professional growth as clinicians.

If we feel that a trainee had a particularly intense presentation we will reach out by the end of the day to check in with them and offer our support. We clarify from the start that we are always available for support and processing beyond class time. Trainees know that they can contact us, and we are accessible and willing to help in between classes.

7. How do we handle trainees who are in crisis or are emotionally unstable?

As described in question 6, we make ourselves available to our trainees throughout the duration of the program, not only during classes but in between classes and whenever they need us for support and processing. When we have a trainee in crisis we have to determine whether we can help the trainee navigate the crisis or whether it is something that requires professional help. In the latter case, we will help the trainee connect with a therapist outside the school.

8. How do we handle trainees who shut down or become very defensive during their presentation?

We take a step back and connect with their fear and the wall, we use the same skills we are teaching the trainees to use with clients, and reach down into ourselves to look for similar experiences that will help us empathize with their need to shut down and protect themselves. We reach out to them and connect through talking about their fear. We help them accept their need to put up a wall, and try to figure out how this need was developed. It also becomes another learning experience about what they will experience with their clients, and how the situation becomes an opportunity to deepen trust in the therapeutic relationship where the client can see the therapist as someone interested in the client's welfare and not in making a point.

9. Why do we always work in pairs? Can this work be done by one facilitator?

The facilitators are usually two, and ideally male and female. We are bringing our own personal selves to the process with the trainees, and with two persons and both genders, we offer a broader set of life perspectives, as well as a choice of support for the trainees as they make themselves vulnerable when dealing with their issues. Usually one of the facilitators takes the lead with a trainee, hoping to make the best match for a particular presentation. Moreover, a responsibility of the two facilitators is to monitor one another's process with the trainees, serving to support, complement and correct one another as indicated by the needs of the trainees. As with the therapist, the work of the facilitators on the "self" is an ever, ongoing process, and our partners in the training are explicitly understood to be a vital part of that effort as related to our performance in the training context.

10. How come what we do is not therapy? It sounds like therapy.

What we do can be therapeutic without being therapy. It can promote personal growth in the process of promoting professional development. What sets the boundary is the goal of the process, which is to make a better therapist—one who can better connect, understand and touch clients therapeutically, however alien from his/her own life experience. This means that many of the skills and techniques we use to achieve that goal with the trainee may be similar to and exactly like those we use as therapists. After all, the essences of our professional tools are based on the common human tools we use to relate, understand and influence people.

Although trainees often report personal growth as a result of the training, the focus of the training is always on making them better therapists and not on resolving their personal issues.

11. How do we make the trainees comfortable with their flaws and vulnerabilities? It is easy to understand the concept of the "wounded healer" but how do we help trainees actually feel and accept it?

We begin by demonstrating that our flaws and vulnerabilities are part of the fabric of common humanity. It is that woundedness that invites empathy and love. The group experience led by the example of the facilitators becomes a context in which the trainees receive support and encouragement, and the chance to offer it to others.

On top of that the trainees learn that it is in how they face and engage their woundedness that they come to better understand themselves and have the opportunity to grow and change. This personal experience leads them to discover that the better they come to understand themselves, and have gained greater access to their inner struggles, the better they will be able to see and feel what their clients are living and struggling with. They will have an incentive not only to "accept" their woundedness, but to "embrace" it as the medium through which they will grow personally and professionally.

12. To what extent are we requiring the trainees to expose themselves?

We tell the trainees that they can share as much as they feel comfortable sharing. We also tell them that we are more interested in their reactions to their life experiences than in the specific details of any event. We validate the extent they are willing to go to in sharing of themselves and express our appreciation of their courage to expose themselves in front of us and their classmates. As the training progresses, trainees see that the more risk they take, the more we are able to help them make effective use of themselves in their clinical work because they are making more of themselves available to all aspects of the therapeutic process. Also, with time and with witnessing their classmates being vulnerable, most trainees feel more comfortable sharing themselves and are willing to take the risk and become vulnerable in class. They learn that personal risk can be rewarded with professional development.

13. Do we practice what we preach? Do we talk to trainees about our own signature themes, flaws and vulnerabilities?

We do, with targeted purpose—economically and prudently. If they need something of our own stories to cross a bridge we cannot help them do through their own experience or the borrowed experience of another trainee's story, we will share a personal or professional anecdote—only to the extent we judge necessary to help them across. We do not want to distract them from the lessons of their own journeys. If ours can help them better connect to their own, and not detract from the roles we must maintain with them, we will share.

14. How do we maintain clear boundaries with trainees to make sure the training doesn't turn into therapy?

We always keep in mind that our goal is not to solve the trainees' personal problems but to teach them how to be effective therapists. Our focus is always on how they can use what they learn about themselves to help their clients. Even if during a presentation or a simulated case we go into a personal issue, we always connect it to the trainee's clinical work and the ultimate goal of effectively using the self to connect, assess and intervene with clients. That is also why it is important that during training the greater proportion of the time is spent working with clinical material, which gives them repeated experiences of thinking about and practicing how to apply what they are learning about themselves to their clinical work. We also emphasize the importance of seeking post-training supervision to help them continue to evolve in their skills of the use of self in therapy.

15. How do we prepare for the trainees' presentations?

We read the presenters' written materials, and meet each week before the trainees present whether on their signature themes or their cases. We look to identify themes in the trainee's write-up, think about how to approach these themes and which of us should take the lead in the discussion with the trainee, considering which of us is the best match for that trainee, on that theme and in that point of the trainee's training.

16. How do we prepare for the simulated therapy sessions?

The co-facilitators refresh themselves on the trainee's signature theme, and how it may present itself in the trainee's clinical work. In our meeting before the simulated family session we try to anticipate what the trainee will need from us to maximize the benefit he or she may gain from the experience with the particular simulated family he or she will work with. We also consider which of us may be best suited to deliver the message, and how it may best be delivered. The aim is to have the experience with the family be the teacher, more than that the trainee will gain some new intellectual insight from us. The POTT class looks to bring both new insight and new experience to the trainee so that the "class" will be more of a "training" than a traditional didactic class.

The POTT class begins as a didactic experience, and evolves over time into a clinical training. The students need to learn the theory and philosophy behind the clinical skills we aim to help them develop. However, as the class progresses, it becomes more clinically experiential. We want them to see themselves in the clinical process, and to experience themselves as the key tool in the implementation of the technical training in the mastery of their clinical skills.

7 Integrating POTT into Your Setting

Applications and Modifications

Karni Kissil and Harry J. Aponte

In this book we describe in detail the implementation of the POTT model in the training of master's students at the Department of Couple and Family Therapy in Drexel University. We realize that not all settings are similar and able to structure the training the same way it is structured at the Drexel program. Therefore, in this chapter we describe possible adaptations of POTT to various settings and facilities, and include the nuts and bolts involved in implementing POTT in different settings. We answer questions such as "how do we use POTT without a simlab?" "how do we train actors to play clients?" and "can POTT be used as a model for peer supervision"? To make it easier for the reader to find the relevant information, we present the information in a format of questions and answers.

1. We don't have a simlab in our setting. Can we still incorporate POTT?

There are several modifications you can apply to incorporate POTT without using a simlab. First, you can use actors in a regular classroom and have the rest of the students sit at the end of the class. When the supervisor pauses the session, he/she and the student, playing therapist, can leave the classroom out of ear shot of those playing the clients, and after their discussion come back to the session. In this scenario, you need a budget to pay the actors. In the next two, you will not. Second, if your setting is part of a college or university, you can recruit students that need extra credit and offer credit for participating as actors. It is important to make sure you have the actors for a full semester or several weeks because we want the trainees to get a sense of the therapeutic process and go beyond the first session. Third, you can create simulated clients by using other students in the class to role-play clients. You can then supervise the student, playing therapist, by freezing the action, and while staying in the classroom ask the student to reflect on what he/she sees in the therapeutic process so far at a professional level (analyzing what is happening at the moment and suggesting the appropriate therapeutic action), and then at a personal level (speaking to personal reactions and associations to what is happening, and giving voice to how he/she may use "self" next in relating, understanding and/or intervening in the moment). In all these scenarios, you can ask the student/therapist to bring a video camera and record the session so he/she can go back and reflect about the session.

2. How do we prepare the actors to play clients in therapy?

There are two ways to do so. If we work with actors hired to play a family or a couple, we come up with a background story around an issue we would like our trainees to work with (e.g. infidelity, parenting or addiction). We meet with the actors and provide them with the background story. Below we offer an example. As you can see, we sketch the background story, but expect the actors to fill out the details extemporaneously as so moved. For example, we don't decide what kind of jobs the couple has. We let the actors build their own characters. We also don't structure the process of therapy because we want the actors to be authentic, and go with how they are personally moved as they get into their roles with each other and the therapist. We want our trainees to have a realistic experience of the kind of clients they will meet in the outside world. The more the actors get into their roles and play authentically, the better our trainees can resonate with and intuit where their client/actors genuinely are, which is the primary goal of the POTT training. Below are two example scripts used one in each of our classes to prepare the actors. We aim to offer some experience of diversity for the students, who themselves come from diverse racial and ethnic backgrounds.

Case #1: Caucasian Family

Mother, father and daughter appear for the first session. The daughter (17), an only child, has been showing troubling behaviors in the past several months. She has been cutting classes and her grades have deteriorated. She had been a straight A student until this past year and very involved in after-school activities. The parents also caught her smoking pot on two occasions and they suspect more extensive use. They don't like her new friends who are taking up too much of her time. She is irritable, easily triggered and is isolating herself when home. She keeps telling them that she is fine and to leave her alone, but they suspect a hidden problem. The parents are both in their mid-forties, are caring but also busy in their careers, and in a conflictual relationship.

Case #2: African-American Couple

The husband and wife are in their late forties, middle class and with two children who are now away at Penn State. They are both teachers, she in middle school and he in high school. This is their first year without children at home. She is busy teaching and taking classes for her doctorate. She pressures him to come in because she believes he has a drinking problem, something he denies. She is also unhappy because he is not showing much interest in her. He resents her "nagging."

After the session, the actors privately discuss among themselves what kind of feedback they want to offer the student, following an outline that addresses

Table 7.1 Guidelines for actors' feedback for the therapist

Questions about the person of the therapist	Feedback on building the relationship	Feedback on assessment	Feedback on intervention	What questions do you have for us?
What did you most like about working with us?	What we liked most about how you related to us	What made us feel most understood by you	What we found most helpful about your work with us	
What did you find most challenging about working with us?	What we liked least about how you related to us	What made us feel least understood by you	What we found least helpful about your work with us	

the relationship, assessment and intervention with the clients. The outline they follow is given in Table 7.1.

When we use our own students as clients, we use a different approach. We have the students choose their roles and ages in the family or couple they wish to play, and then ask them not to consult one another about the issue that brings them in, but to invent the issue extemporaneously and their respective perspectives on it independently of one another thereby forcing them to generate the dynamics of their relationship around the issue as they feel it. Again, what we are looking for is that the players, whether professionals or student volunteers, play what they actually feel so that the student therapist is reacting to something that they experience as authentic.

The supervision of this process aims for a different learning experience for the student who plays the therapist and for the others who are observing. The purpose is to teach the student therapist to identify, monitor and manage what is going on within him/herself as he/she works to relate, assess and intervene with the simulated family or couple. The supervisor/s freeze the action at each point where the student therapist must make a significant decision about what direction to go next so the supervisor can offer feedback and guidance about how to use the self in the next therapeutic action. As described above, at the end of the exercise with the supervisor/s, the actors offer informal feedback about how they felt about their experience with the therapist.

3. Do we have to use two trainers for each class?

In an ideal application of the model we have two trainers, preferably a male and a female. As we described in Chapter 6, as facilitators, we bring our own personal selves to the process with the trainees, and with two persons and both genders we offer a broader set of life perspectives, as well as a choice of support for the trainees as they make themselves vulnerable when dealing with their issues. Usually one of the facilitators takes the lead with a trainee, hoping to make the best match for a particular presentation. The match may be by gender, race, ethnicity, age, etc., basically someone with whom you believe the student presenter may feel most comfortable sharing his/her story. Moreover, a responsibility of the two facilitators is to monitor one another's process with the trainees, serving to support, complement and correct one another as indicated by the needs of the trainees. Having said that, we know that in some cases having two facilitators is not feasible. The training can be run by a single person who is experienced in POTT. In these cases we recommend supervision for the facilitator by a supervisor who is trained in POTT.

The best way to become a POTT instructor is to first go through the experience as a trainee, and then become a co-trainer with an experienced POTT instructor. After having implemented POTT for the first time in an institution, previous trainees become potential co-trainers. This way, a trainer that has led the class individually, at first, can recruit a co-trainer among previous trainees. It is important to keep in mind that the selection of a co-trainer has to be thoughtful to avoid dual relationships. For example, if the training is offered in an academic setting, it would be advisable for the new co-trainer to have graduated from the program or be at a different level than the students being trained (e.g. a doctoral student co-training a POTT class in a master's level program).

4. We are a big private practice and we would like to use POTT for our peer group supervision. How can we do that?

It is not advisable to encourage peers to share their private life experiences with one another, especially when they are in a professional working relationship. The process requires a leader who not only guides the process toward greater and clinically relevant insight, but also maintains safe boundaries for those exploring and discussing any personal material in relation to cases. The supervisor can guide professionals in group-supervision in speaking to their signature themes in general terms (e.g. "I tend to avoid conflict") without revealing personal historical details (e.g. "I was physically abused as a child"), while also ensuring that the discussion is strictly related to the case under consideration. The participants can present cases and speak to how they personally react to and feel about the clients and their issues when they believe their personal reactions may be influencing how they relate and work with the clients. The supervisor needs to help clinicians identify not only when and how their personal reactions may impede their effectiveness with clients, but also how they may be able to use themselves purposefully and actively to enhance how they relate, assess and intervene with particular clients and their issues. The supervisor is responsible for keeping the participants conscious of the importance of being prudent about what they reveal of themselves to the colleagues with whom they will be working in various capacities on the job.

5. We are a therapy center that wants to conduct an intensive group training or supervision once a month. Can the POTT model fit into that schedule or does it have to be on a weekly basis?

Some service centers have several branches, and bring staff from various locations together on a monthly basis for a training experience. In those instances one or two or more supervisory sessions following any of the above models can be used for supervision of the presenting therapist as well as a teaching experience for the observing staff. In that case the supervisor of the therapist is doubling as the teacher for the bigger group that is observing, or one person can serve as a supervisor and a second person the teacher. Because it is an in-house training, a live family session can be the subject of supervision. To avoid a theater-type environment for the family or couple, the session should be conducted on the other side of a two-way mirror or through a closed-circuit TV transmission. If the client family or couple is being seen live, the supervision needs to be as unobtrusive as possible to avoid disrupting the therapeutic flow of the session. When a live family is the subject of the experience, ethically their wellbeing must be the primary concern of those overseeing the training/supervisory session.

Because of the relative personal nature of the POTT supervision, the supervision group should be as stable in membership and attendance as possible. We recommend asking participants to commit to a specific number of sessions to maintain stability for the group and facilitate the creation of a safe place for members. Respect for the personal vulnerability of the individual being supervised and confidentiality for any personal material shared by the clinician should be observed.

6. I am an independent supervisor providing individual and group supervision for therapists. Can I use POTT in my individual and group supervision?

Circumstances where the therapists receiving supervision have not undergone the full POTT training experience cannot provide the same kind of POTT-based supervision as those whose supervisees have undergone the training. They have not been guided through an experience where they identify their signature themes in an environment where they are helped to be prudent about how much and what kind of personal information they share. Nor have they been trained on how to make a planned active use of their personal characteristics, social background and life experience in the implementation of their clinical tools whatever their therapeutic orientation may be. Essentially supervision where supervisee and supervisor are fully trained in the model allows for continued work on understanding the supervisee's signature theme in relation to the latter's clinical work, while in supervision where that training in the POTT model is lacking, the supervisor only addresses personal material about the therapist to the extent it directly relates to the specific case on hand. The privacy of the supervisee needs to be respected and protected. The full-scale training model is structured to be a safe place to be vulnerable about exploring personal information to gain greater understanding of it so that the trainee can work on gaining mastery of self within the clinical context. The purely supervisory structure is meant to guide supervisees in mining what they know of themselves and have access of themselves strictly within the boundaries of their work with particular clients.

7. The program in Drexel is offered two hours a week for a full academic year. We can only offer it for one semester in our academic program, three hours a week. Is it still worth doing?

It is always potentially worthwhile, but you must adapt the goals and methods of training to the resources and limitations of your setting. Below we describe how the POTT model has been modified to fit in weekly three-hour sessions during a 16-week semester. In this model, the maximum number of students who could be accommodated and receive the full POTT experience was nine (or ten if an extra weekly meeting is scheduled). Under these circumstances, the students will get:

- An introduction to the POTT philosophy—two weeks.
- The signature theme presentations—three students per week for three weeks.
- The case presentation and the simlab experience—one of each weekly for nine weeks.
- The closing presentation—five and four presentations respectively in the last two weeks.

For a lower number of participants, the instructors and trainees can decide how to better allocate the remainder of the time (e.g. offer students the opportunity to have a second case presentation, have a second round of signature theme presentations). For groups of more than ten participants, it is recommended to divide the group into two sections.

It is important to keep in mind that POTT sessions are emotionally demanding for the trainees as well as the trainers. Offering the training in weekly two-hour sessions for nine months requires students and trainees a lower weekly demand and more time in the academic year for emotional processing when compared to the more condensed semester version. For that reason, trainees and trainers need to actively invest in self-care methods. In addition, trainers should make themselves available for trainees beyond the session time for processing of their reactions to the class.

8. In order to benefit mostly from the training, what kind of equipment do we need?

Because in the POTT model therapists are expected to be particularly aware of self in both the personal and professional dimensions of the clinical performance, there needs to be a capability to observe live and to record therapists' performance with their clients. Observation rooms with two-way mirrors, closed-circuit TV and videotaping capacity for groups in training and individuals in supervision are all equipment and facilities optimal from one or another aspect of training or supervision. Trainers, supervisors and the therapists themselves all need to be able to see the therapist in action. There is too much that happens in the personal interaction between clinician and client for any therapist or supervisor/trainer to be totally dependent on therapist self-reporting from memory. Videotaping sessions allows therapists to go back and watch their clinical sessions as many times as they wish, and reflect on their own process (how they felt, what they thought and what they did at any specific moment of engagement with clients). Trainers and supervisors need equipment that permits them to observe and to demonstrate because the human interaction is so complex that simple reporting has value for discussion, but one that is limited when it comes to evaluating and guiding action in the multi-level and multi-dimensional dynamics of the human relational system between a therapist and his/her clients. The therapeutic process is not just a conversation between people, but more fully a human experience within the professional boundaries of a process that beats with a human heart under the guidance of a clinical eye.

8   POTT Principles Across Mental Health Disciplines

"Just Use Your Clinical Judgment"

Jody Russon and Renata Carneiro

Most clinicians remember seeing clients for the very first time. For many of us, these initial clinical encounters were laden with anxieties and uncertainties. The tough decisions, intricate case conceptualizations and ethical problem-solving strategies were overwhelming in the face of entirely new professional responsibilities. Furthermore, we were simultaneously learning that decision-making is rarely a dichotomous process and it requires an analysis of too many viable options. At the end of the day, many of us found that after the clinical notes were scrutinized, the intake forms re-reviewed and the conceptualization discussed again in supervision, the only advice left was to "just use your clinical judgment."

The POTT philosophy and model provide a framework for new clinicians to begin building their clinical judgment as they enter their first professional experiences. As noted in the present text, POTT emphasizes clinical growth through self-knowledge, self-access and self-management. Due to these primary concepts, POTT has the potential to span across mental health disciplines, such as MFT, professional counseling, psychology and social work. For the mental health professions, POTT provides a pathway for clinicians to use their personal experiences as core therapeutic resources. The more connected professionals are to their own personal life challenges and personal relationships, the more they have of themselves available to enrich and deepen the wisdom, sensitivity and intuition of their professional performance. The active, conscious and purposeful use of their life experiences—the good and the bad—can better attune them to the personal experience of their clients along with the immediate and present unfolding of the therapeutic relationship, helping to inform the complex process of therapists' clinical judgment.

Because of its connection to the universal human condition of the therapist, the POTT model is an approach that is applicable across mental health disciplines. This chapter's specific aims include the following: (1) understanding the importance of clinical judgment as defined by the POTT philosophy; (2) demonstrating the usefulness of the POTT model for developing clinical judgment; and (3) demonstrating the model's applicability to practice-related standards in the various fields of mental health.

Defining Clinical Judgment in the Context of POTT

Although perspectives on clinical judgment have evolved over time, all mental health professions promote concepts associated with clinical judgment as crucial elements for initiating therapeutic change for diverse individuals, families and communities (AAMFT, 2005; APA, 2009; CACREP, 2009; COAMFTE, 2013; CSWE, 2008). Recently, clinical judgment has been defined as "the study of therapists' decisions on tasks such as assessment, diagnosis, problem definition, case conceptualization, prognosis, and intervention" (Jankowski et al., 2012, p. 17). Many believe that clinical judgment is an ability that develops over time—seeing clients, conceptualizing cases and experiencing human nature and its diversity in the context of therapy (Ægisdóttir et al., 2006). Indeed, studies have shown that experienced clinicians are able to make more accurate diagnoses and reliable treatments than novice therapists (Garb, 1989, 1994; Spengler et al., 2009). The POTT perspective takes this observation to imply that with professional experience also comes personal life experience, all of which potentially adds wisdom to professional judgment.

When defining the practice of clinical judgment, the POTT model emphasizes the influence of the universal human experience, and, in particular, the painful experiences of life (Aponte & Kissil, 2014). Accordingly, POTT embraces the practice of understanding oneself, the clinician, as a "wounded healer" (Nouwen, 1979), and uses this frame when forming a relationship, assessing and intervening with clients (Aponte, 1994; Aponte & Winter, 2013). This framework facilitates an isomorphic process of self-awareness and self-acceptance in therapists that can encourage clients, verbally and non-verbally, to accept their own emotional vulnerabilities as a portal of possibility—reaching deep within one's self and into one's relationships for deeper understanding and strength toward a renewed self.

As clinicians, we can agree that we all have unique life experiences and, therefore, have personally distinct abilities to connect, assess and intervene with clients. POTT encourages clinicians to achieve insight into the humanness of their clients through their connection to their own personal struggles, unique in their particular experience, but universal in their humanity. It is this personal resonance with clients that allows for the instinctive ability to use interpersonal reactions and interactions with clients to intuit unarticulated data about the client, hidden in the content discussed in session. Without the ability of therapists to readily access in the moment, in session, their own inner personal experience they lose: (1) the capacity to capture clients' painful experiences to the fullest (enabled by intuition) and (2) the potential to enter with the client into that intimate human connection that fosters trust and openness to change (Satir, 2013).

A Metaphor for Training

The POTT model helps clinicians develop their clinical judgment by emphasizing the importance of the use of self as a fundamental instrument of therapeutic work. Like actors, clinicians use their own emotions to understand the affective experiences of clients. For example, when an actress is studying a character, she draws from her own experiences to portray the character in a profoundly personal way. Drawing upon these experiences, she then can replicate her character's experience with authenticity. This organic process, portrayed by the actress on stage, gives her character genuine credibility. In order to accurately portray the experience of someone else, who may be completely different from herself, the actress must actively inquire about her character's emotional experience to understand it from within herself; she then draws from her own emotional toolbox to immerse herself in the character's depiction. This is of the utmost importance because even though the actress and character may come from different backgrounds and have distinct personal experiences, life's challenges and contretemps are a universal part of the human experience, which, however different, will always have some points of resonance from one party to another. It is this common human core that enables the clinician to resonate deeply and authentically with the client's personal struggles.

The actress must actively place herself in the position of the other. For instance, if she is required to play an alcoholic and has never had a drink in her life, she must find an aspect of the alcoholic's experience she can relate to, such as the desperate need to escape from some painful component of life. She will try to see life, people and interactions from the standpoint of her character, ask questions about her character's experiences and strive to interpret the inner forces of this character with which she can identify. Now is the time that she must reflect on and connect with her own life experiences that enable her to resonate emotionally with this character. Furthermore, she can use these reactions to drive her questions about her character, and fill in the missing pieces of the story line. As she becomes experienced, she learns how to have her reactions work for her, however subtle or intense, pleasant or painful they may be. With time, the actress develops a distinctive intuitive capacity to resource her own life experiences to resonate with a character's life experiences, however different they appear from her own.

Like the actress in the example, clinicians must immerse themselves in clients' stories by actively listening and searching for personal experiences of their own that can aid in connecting to the client. The clinician then can carefully select particular personal experiences that can fuel questions and statements for assessment and intervention. By accessing her personal experiences, not only of the past, but also of the present in her interactions with the client, the clinician can use her reactions to guide her pacing and attunement to the client. Using the universal language of emotion to open a connection with client, the clinician learns to use her life experience to inform the process of her therapeutic work.

Developing Clinical Judgment Through POTT

POTT can serve as a guide for integrating the development of clinical judgment and use of self in the training of therapists. As a mechanism of using oneself in the therapeutic encounter, clinical judgment is an intellectual process punctuated by the therapist's personal insight into a client's experience, which can direct clinicians with greater attunement to a client's personal processes. Clinical judgment informed by the therapist's own personal resonance with the client's emotional processes helps clinicians determine answers to situational decisions, like when to intervene and how therapy should be paced. They need to know how to actively use their own personal experiences as a constructive tool instead of allowing the intensity or their reactions or sensitivity to overwhelm or disengage them when triggered in a clinical encounter. As with the actress in the aforementioned example, this honing of skills takes practice and instruction. In the POTT model, clinicians' life circumstances and struggles are framed as resources in establishing points of connection with clients. In this way, like actors find their roles in their characters, clinicians "find their clients in themselves" (Aponte, 1994, p. 4).

Practice-Related Standards

The implementation of clinical judgment has been an elusive concept in many academic and clinical settings. At present, understanding the process of teaching clinical judgment is vague in educational literature, leaving trainees with little practical assistance in the development of clinical judgment (Ivey et al., 1999). Clinicians are responsible for the task of investigating clients' behavioral, emotional and cognitive presentations, while encouraging growth through support and therapeutic challenge. These skills require practice in self-management and sensitivity. Although a host of guides and protocols are being consistently developed, scholars have argued that clinicians rarely have direct guidance on how to personally process clinical information (Ivey et al., 1999).

Professionals are often attuned to identifying patterns in behaviors, emotions or thoughts in their clients. Furthermore, many therapeutic approaches, across disciplines, have also incorporated clients' cultural identities as a focal point (Freshwater, 2003; Smith et al., 2006). These approaches have emphasized the importance of becoming sensitive to environmental contexts and human diversity. They reinforce the notion that humans, as relational beings, are affected by their families and communities, as well as by broader environmental and social forces. With this said, scholars are increasingly emphasizing the importance of developing clinical judgment as one way to encourage professional growth in understanding clients' interpersonal, social and societal contexts (Ivey et al., 1999; Jankowski et al., 2012).

Accrediting Organizations

Within present day educational settings, the development of clinical judgment seems to be a component of training to be developed upon engagement in actual clinical practice. This means that trainees have little opportunity to practice exercising their clinical judgment until they find themselves face-to-face with clients. Most trainees experience a fair amount of anxiety about exercising clinical judgment when first beginning to work in the field (Gelman, 2004). In order to better equip trainees to engage effectively with clients, we need to articulate a solid framework for understanding the development of clinical judgment.

Accreditation organizations recognize that therapeutic change stems from interventions originating from the clinician (APA, 2009; CACREP, 2009; COAMFTE, 2013; CSWE, 2008); thus, the clinician is seen as a *change agent*. The POTT model applies directly to training criteria across the various mental health disciplines by facilitating the development of clinical judgment. As described in this book (see Chapter 1), the POTT model addresses three areas of self-work (self-knowledge, self-access and self-management) in the three components of action of therapy (relationship, assessment and intervention). These concepts allow the clinician to conduct each part of the therapeutic process with a deeper personal understanding of the client's experiences. Similarly, all clinical-related standards address developing competence in the following areas of practice: clinical preparation, assessment and diagnosis, and intervention. These standards further reiterate that clinical competence requires a basis of experience executing sound clinical judgments specific to each area of therapeutic practice.

Examining the POTT Process

In order to guide the client in this process of self-understanding and change, POTT emphasizes the constant interaction between differentiation and identification (Lutz & Irizarry, 2009). These processes enable the clinician's stance, vis-à-vis the client, to shift as therapeutically necessary. This allows for the clinician to create powerful, emotional experiences with the client while maintaining a dual stance: being fully present with the client in the moment while, at the same time, taking a more differentiated, scientific perspective on the complexity of the case's process (Aponte & Kissil, 2014). This duality necessitates a heightening of clinical judgment as the fully present personal self seeks to resonate with the complexities of the clients' experiences, while the professional self organizes this information into an active therapeutic plan of intervention.

The crux of the POTT model relies on understanding personal themes associated with key core issues. This provides clinicians with a chance to exercise greater mastery over their personal selves while conducting therapeutic tasks (Aponte & Carlsen, 2009). POTT has demonstrated the capacity to be integrated in both educational and institutional settings for training therapists (Aponte et al., 2009, Aponte & Kissil, 2014). Thus far, the model has been incorporated into an MFT program and a private clinical practice (Aponte et al., 2009). In these locations, the model has become a crucial part of promoting clinicians' readiness for the discerning complexities of clinical work. It has promoted trainees learning to accept and work actively with and through their human struggles, which increases their freedom from the control their personal issues have over their performance as professionals (Aponte & Carlsen, 2009).

The prism of one's inner experience serves the clinician as a personal medium through which clients' life experiences can be captured and interpreted. This, in turn, aids in case formulation, evaluation and intervention. Beginning clinicians have consistently reported on the helpfulness of these principles (Aponte et al., 2009; Niño et al., 2013).

POTT teaches clinicians to flexibly respond to clients' unique personal processes and social contexts. As aforementioned, the model's principles of self-work (self-knowledge, self-access and self-management) promote competence in all areas of therapeutic practice as outlined by organizational accreditation standards relating to preparation, assessment and diagnosis, and intervention. The following sections address: (1) how the POTT principles of self-work map onto each area of therapeutic practice; (2) how these components of action are informed by the POTT principles of self-work; and (3) how the interactions between these principles of self-work and components of action create a framework for clinical judgment.

Excerpts from a POTT trainee's class papers (one of the authors—JR) will be included to demonstrate an example of personal processing within each section of this educational structure. In addition, POTT supervision commentary, provided by Harry Aponte, will be included as part of the description. Although the vignettes will provide examples of the interactions between the components of action and principles of self-work within a stage-like structure of preparation, it is important to emphasize that these interactions do not occur in a linear pattern within the POTT model. Just as the therapeutic process involves the weaving of preparation, assessment and diagnosis, along with intervention techniques throughout its course, the POTT action components and principles of self-work are active throughout the clinical encounters. Furthermore, the vignettes only present a couple of examples of the multiple ways POTT can be used for developing clinical judgment during preparation, assessment and diagnosis, and intervention.

Clinical Preparation

When considering how to recognize clinical judgment and preparedness, it is important to understand the basics of creating a therapeutic environment. A basic common factor of all therapies and treatment approaches involves the development and maintenance of a therapeutic relationship (Lambert & Ogles, 2004; Sprenkle et al., 2009; Wampold, 2010). Clinicians must have the relational tools to facilitate empathetic interventions in order to promote a strong working alliance and solid basis for growth and change. They must have the verbal and non-verbal ability to communicate an understanding of clients' presenting concerns and sensitivities. POTT training enables clinicians to visualize their own struggles in order to establish an empathic relationship with clients. The model facilitates clinicians' development of their clinical judgment by encouraging them to use their personal experiences—historical and in the immediacy of the current clinical engagement—to access and understand those of their clients. This opens clinicians for more possibilities of relating to their clients and creating a space for personally authentic interactions. The experiential connection forms the foundational groundwork for maintaining a working relationship.

Beginning clinicians may struggle with the meaning of the therapeutic relationship and how to manage both their professional and personal selves in session (Aponte et al., 2009). The principles of self-knowledge, access and management allow trainees to intersect their roles into a holistic, genuine therapist identity. Expanding self-knowledge encourages clinicians to investigate the experiences that inform their worldviews, while self-access puts them in touch with both emotions and life-perspectives, and with self-management they take all this into account in how they relate to themselves and others— activating their personal selves within their professional roles.

With this said, it is noteworthy that the various accreditation organizations stress the importance of personal and professional preparedness throughout a whole range of areas. For example, some organizations include joining and therapeutic rapport as standards, while others focus more on conducting preparatory work, becoming aware of ethics, and knowing social and legal responsibilities (APA, 2009; CACREP, 2009; COAMFTE, 2013; CSWE, 2008). When addressing clinical preparation, many standards stress the importance of being attuned to the profession in order to provide the groundwork for competent care. This includes understanding intake information as it relates both to individual and systemic data (COAMFTE, 2013), awareness of the role of the clinician and other professionals affiliated with the case (CACREP, 2009), being familiar with theoretical approaches to treatment (APA, 2009) and developing the therapeutic relationship (CSWE, 2008).

The POTT principle of self-knowledge allows for clinicians' self-awareness; self-access connects that self-awareness to the therapists' actual experiences in session; and self-management enables therapists to develop a working relationship with themselves as professional resources, and put into practice the negotiating of both the personal and scientific selves in session. This prepares therapists to be more fully available personally and professionally to clients in the therapeutic relationship. While organizational standards expect clinicians to recognize their personal biases, POTT takes this a step further and trains clinicians to not just keep these biases out of the way, but to be able to use them in positive ways to recognize, connect with and utilize the values and worldviews of their clients in the therapeutic process. Self-knowledge, access and management provide the groundwork for organizing the soundness and accuracy required in formulating appropriate clinical judgments in their guidance of the work of therapy.

TRAINEE CASE EXAMPLE: SIGNATURE THEME

I (Jody Russon) am a therapist who has been trained in both individual and systemic clinical modalities. The excerpts included throughout the remainder of the chapter represent my personal work over approximately four months in POTT training, with Harry Aponte. The following is an excerpt from my first paper, the signature theme paper (see Chapter 2). This first paper, on the trainee's *signature theme*, served as an initial step for recognizing my own struggles and how they allow me to understand the perspectives and experiences of other human beings.

I struggle with being myself because I do not want others to have the chance to reject me based on who I am. The fear of rejection always shakes my core. I am not used to being rejected because I never let myself relax enough to make a mistake, say something that others do not want to hear, or react emotionally when it does not fit into the expectations of others. I struggle because I am so used to molding myself into what others want me to be that, sometimes, I have difficulties understanding how I feel. I recognize that my choices, interpersonal behaviors, and driving feelings are associated and, perhaps, dictated by my signature theme: the fear that I am not worthy of love and simply not good enough. This same fear motivates me to please others.

I have recognized the emergence of my signature theme in my clinical work thus far. For example, when a client is not progressing, I become anxious because I fear that I am not helping enough. If a client is not happy with me or does not agree with an intervention, it shakes my feeling of competence. Moreover, I do have a tendency to have more anxiety about confronting clients as the therapeutic relationship develops because I do not want to cause the client's trust in me to diminish. I also worry about the possibility of the client leaving therapy all together.

POTT supervisory feedback (HA): Jody demonstrates a painful awareness of how her signature theme impacts her in her personal and professional relationships, as well as her relationship to herself. From her first paper, it is clear that she lacks confidence in her ability to really connect with the core of her clients' issues. In her fear that she will be rejected as a therapist and as a person, she so tries to please the client that she struggles to connect with her own emotions. We will begin by helping Jody to investigate her theme further. We will ask Jody to talk about why it is so frightening to be rejected. We want her to get in touch within herself with the sources of these fears, in a way that will foster her empathy for this part of her struggle. This understanding of and ability to articulate for herself the story behind this fear of rejection and consequent need to please will help her gain some distance from and perspective on how difficult is this very common human issue. This is the beginning of freeing herself from viewing her issue as segregating her from others, and instead, viewing her personal struggle with her insights into it as a bridge to understanding and empathizing with others, in particular her clients.

The more Jody opens herself to the breadth of her experiences, the more comfortable she will feel resonating with her clients' struggles. The more sensitively she attunes herself to her client, the more available will be her intuition to inform the observational data needed to formulate her clinical judgment. As Jody's level of attunement to her clients' shared human struggles grows, so will her ability to determine the manner of relating to the needs of her clients.

She will learn how to use her personal woundedness constructively instead of locking herself up in shame and fear because of her human vulnerabilities.

Assessment and Diagnosis

Competence in assessment and diagnosis requires that clinicians are able to accurately identify the issues and contextual complexities that clients bring into therapy. All accreditation organizations address building aptitude for clinical assessment through diagnostic evaluation and observation. Educational standards promote competencies in assessment and diagnosis by requiring that programs build students' knowledge and skills in areas such as etiology, measurement tools and interpersonal observation. This includes identifying patterns in relational behavior (COAMFTE, 2013), knowing concepts of disease and prevention (CACREP, 2009), diagnosing through intentional assessment approaches (APA, 2009) and being aware of clients' personal strengths and limitations (CSWE, 2008). POTT training fosters not only self-awareness, but also a ready access to therapists' inner experience of their issues/themes in the clinical moment to facilitate the therapist's ability to read the client not only with eyes and ears, but also with the intuitive insights gathered from the inner resonance to the client's struggles. The usefulness of these skills is particularly relevant during assessment as they provide the added lens of the therapist's resonating humanity for investigating the experiences, thought processes and emotions of the client.

Once the interactions between self-awareness/access and assessment are well understood, clinicians are taught to balance the processes of identification and differentiation throughout therapeutic contacts (Aponte et al., 2009). In these dichotomous processes, clinicians are encouraged to connect to the commonalities between their own experiences and the clients' while grounded in their own distinct life's journey. As aforementioned, this selective identification and differentiation opens the clinician for engagement on a deeper level with clients' issues while facilitating the distance needed to keep clinical perspective on the case (Aponte & Kissil, 2014). As clinical judgment, by definition, focuses on the process of clinicians' decision-making (Jankowski et al., 2012), professionals gain greater mastery in organizing information directly learned from the client and intuited about the client. In sum, the professional self within this very human therapeutic relationship provides a basis for an efficient way to identify the essence of clients' concerns in the interest of better assessment and diagnosis.

TRAINEE CASE EXAMPLE: FIRST CASE PRESENTATION

The following excerpt is from my first *case presentation* paper where I reflect on my signature theme with regard to a clinical case. My writing demonstrates how I use both identification and differentiation to develop a hypothesis about the case. I describe how I access some of the emotions surrounding my own signature theme that also relate to the client's situation in order to gain insights into the case. This process aids in my clinical judgment about the client's issues.

K, a 16-year-old adolescent boy, initially attended therapy individually because of disabling anxiety. K had been engaged in a process of avoiding anxiety-provoking situations for a number of years. When I spoke with his dad briefly on the phone he reported some periods of school refusal. K's therapeutic goal was to work through his anxiety and fear in order to attend school on a regular basis and be successful. He was in the 11th grade and hoped to graduate high school "on time" in approximately one more year. K stated that he felt a need to talk with his dad when he felt worried or fearful, but he expressed a desire to be more self-sufficient so he could take full advantage of school and social opportunities. K reported that his worry had held him back from engaging in activities at school. He was particularly afraid of "making a fool" of himself in front of classmates, "losing friends," and "saying something stupid."

K's experience with anxiety and avoidance mirrored my own, especially when I was younger. Listening to K's fear about losing his friends reminded me of my profound fear of rejection by others. Hearing K's description of sitting alone in the locker room because he was too nervous to try out for baseball made me think of how I wanted to be deemed highly by others at all times and how paralyzing this was for me. Like me, K did not give himself any mercy when it came to his fears about how others would perceive him. It was sad for me to hear that others made fun of him in school by calling him a "weirdo." Like myself, he was also determined, at all costs, to get the best grades. This too made me think of the over-achieving cycle that exists within me. I often overwork to show myself and others that I am not worthless and that I do, indeed, deserve to be loved. For K, it seemed like this was the only power he felt like he had access to.

After our first session, I found I could relate to K's experience of feeling "not okay" with himself almost all the time. I learned that his household was emotionally chaotic, and that his relationship with his dad was close, but highly conflictual. K's dad was a single parent and worked at a high-paced job to support himself and his son. K's mom moved out when K was four years old. She had not kept in contact with K or his dad. K's dad was not in our first session, and K offered that he thought his dad was "too busy." From K's descriptions, his dad seemed to be constantly overwhelmed and exhausted from his job, and was not able to be a consistent source of emotional support to K. In many ways, I felt that K was often expected to make emotional sense out of the chaos and stress in the household.

I had an interesting reaction to K. When I feel as though I can too easily identify with someone, I tend to pull back and remain professional. I do this because I am afraid to let my personal self get in the way of my professional responsibilities. I noticed that K did not stay with his emotional experience in session either, and considered this might have been due to the fact that I never made space for it. He may have perceived me as a helper or a type of coach, but not a therapist who could provide him with a place where his emotions can be held. I am not sure I provide that space for myself either at times. My relationship with myself is like a coach instead of a nurturing healer, yet I want to be a nurturing, healing therapist.

POTT supervisory feedback (HA): Jody explores how she can use her own struggles as a tool for developing her clinical voice. During the case presentation, we interjected and asked Jody about her struggle between being a coach and wanting to be a healing therapist in this clinical instance. The goal was to explore her experience of silencing and not trusting her intuition (thus limiting the use of her clinical judgment). Jody reported feeling paralyzed. Sensing the pervasiveness of her anxiety, we worked to slow Jody down to allow her to get in touch with her emotions at that moment of her "paralysis." We wanted her to "feel" rather than to "explain." Then, we broke this silence by asking Jody now that she was in touch with her fears to think of K and his fears. Here, we were encouraging Jody to use herself (emotions and experiences) to establish a connection with her client, first within herself. She was able to do that, but when it came to approaching K directly about his anxieties, Jody responded that she was afraid of losing K as a client. Although she felt that she could connect with his experiences emotionally, she was afraid of saying something wrong or pushing him too far. She was afraid that, ultimately, she would lose him as a client and that this would confirm her fears of being "not good enough."

Overall, in this case presentation Jody described how her signature theme was playing out in her relationship with K. She was able to articulate her struggle and how it clouded her clinical judgment to a point where she did not trust herself to attempt to form a real connection with her client. We encouraged her to stay in touch with the resonance she felt with K, and think about what she would need from a therapist to feel safe to talk about her fears, working with what was helping her in her discussion with us at that moment. Her own struggles were becoming a point of connection with her client rather than an impediment to her clinical work.

Intervention

The purpose of the POTT principle of self-management is for clinicians to learn how to project, heighten and lessen selective parts of themselves while engaging clients around their therapeutic tasks (Aponte et al., 2009). Differing from self-disclosure, self-management does not expect a clinician to reveal personal content. Instead, this principle of self-work encourages the therapist to initiate a specific personal stance toward the client related to where the client is at that moment in the therapeutic process to amplify the effectiveness of the intervention. For example, in this case I (JR) might consciously access my fear of personal rejection by my client when trying to convey my understanding and empathy to K about his fear of rejection by his classmates. Instead of addressing K's fears directly, I could describe, with genuine affect rooted in my own self-awareness, how overwhelmingly stressful it might feel for any person with these fears to be pressured to engage with the very people he anticipated would ridicule and reject him. Building upon self-knowledge and self-access, self-management involves the active use of clinical judgment to determine how to implement an intervention.

Accreditation organizations focus on implementation of interventions through therapeutic mechanisms, case management, planning, and prevention techniques. Educational standards promote the creation and ongoing evaluation of interventions that initiate positive changes in clients' behavior, affect, thought processes and relationships. This has included using strategies that suit clients' specific needs and values (COAMFTE, 2013), enabling clients to gain access to community resources (CACREP, 2009), seeking consultation and supervision services to approach clients with well-informed care (APA, 2009) and becoming negotiators, mediators and advocates for clients when the situation requires it (CSWE, 2008). Historically, standards of training across theoretical approaches have required that clinicians gain an awareness of the self to avoid having their personal issues interfere with their therapeutic effectiveness (e.g. the management of countertransference (Freud, 1910), differentiating from family of origin (Kerr & Bowen, 1988)). However, most approaches do not focus on teaching clinicians a defined method of how to use the self with all one's vulnerabilities as a *positive* means of being more empathetic, insightful and effective in therapy, a core principle of the POTT model.

TRAINEE CASE EXAMPLE: SECOND CASE PRESENTATION

The following excerpt is from my second case presentation paper where I incorporated feedback received from my first presentation and followed up on my client (K). I articulate my choice of intervention and method of intervening given my personal awareness of past relationships. I am developing a greater understanding of how I can use myself to execute a more effective strategy with this client. Overall, I explore, with the support of my instructors, how I can use my own struggles as a tool for developing my clinical voice.

K tends to speak minimally and after much thought. In a recent session, he seemed to be working hard to fit into a world that had the potential of rejecting him. This prompted me to communicate my understanding of his situation: "you live in a world of 'what ifs'." This intervention came from my own experience of always worrying that something bad was going to happen to my family or myself.

Part of K did not believe he was strong enough to live up to the challenges that he saw stuck between his reality and his goals. I both identified and differentiated from K's experience with this. I do not have a fear of engaging; instead, my fear stems from letting my vulnerability show. I have been set back by challenges in my life and have a tendency to become overwhelmed in anticipation of failure. Because of this, I found myself wanting K to move out of his own fearful place.

I wanted to continue to ask K questions about his history of attempting to avoid risking failure; however, I sensed his feeling overwhelmed and decided to focus more on the present. I often struggle between wanting to challenge the client and working to build a supportive alliance. Somehow, I felt the need to be more direct with my communication on this occasion, especially about K's avoidance. I directly asked him: "Are you feeling overwhelmed right now?" This forwardness did not feel natural to me at first, but it seemed to establish a safer place for K because of the strength of my connection with him at that moment. I was present with myself and with him in the moment. I felt he knew that I was being attentive to his experience and prioritizing it. I trusted my intuitive judgment, and he responded positively. Specifically, K took a deep breath and said, with tears in his eyes, that he always feels this way and he doesn't know how to make it stop. I listened as he struggled to talk more about how he feels when he is overwhelmed. He said, "my chest tightens and I feel like I can't breathe . . . and there is no one I can go to who can help me . . . I feel all alone." This was new information for me. I had not known before what was going on in K as he struggled silently in our sessions. This gave me a whole new awareness of what K was experiencing and opened me up to connect and work with him in his struggles.

POTT supervisory feedback (HA): At several points in the presentation, we highlighted how Jody had not been afraid of using her clinical judgment to select an experience of her own to connect with K. We supported Jody as she continued to explore K's reaction to her intervention. The goal in that moment was to slow down the process for Jody, encouraging her to reflect and stay connected to her own experiences as she contemplated intervening with K, rehearsing with us what she would want to be doing in the therapy room.

Afterward, Jody reported that she was able to get in touch with her own issues and use them to connect with a depth of understanding that provided her client with a safe space to explore his feelings. She built up the courage to be bold in her directness with him—depending on the immediate reality of their relationship. She was secure enough with her feelings about her connection to K to use her clinical judgment about how and when to intervene. She could feel him and where she was with him as she made her intervention. Overall, Jody's awareness and access to herself, at that moment, gave her the ability to allow her clinical judgment to guide the timing of her interventions. Here, she was able to brave a "forwardness" with her client that was not "natural" to her.

Conclusion

POTT taps into a universal human experience, one that allows for connection through our innate human vulnerabilities. The concepts outlined in this chapter provide the basis for healers, across disciplines, to use their own, valuable personal experiences to connect and work with clients. Their own life experiences and personal reactions in session offer therapists added material by which to better use their clinical judgment in the moment with clients. No matter the setting, POTT reminds us of how vital we, as human beings, are to the work we do if we know how to access and use our personal selves in our professional roles. The POTT philosophy emphasizes the very essence of what we want to help our clients to understand: that acknowledgment and acceptance of human vulnerability creates a pathway for healing and growth.

References

Ægisdóttir, S., White, M.J., Spengler, P.M., Maugherman, A.S., Anderson, L.A., Cook, R.S., et al. (2006). The meta-analysis of clinical judgment project: Fifty-six years of accumulated research on clinical versus statistical prediction. *Counseling Psychologist, 34*(3), 341–382.

AAMFT (American Association for Marriage and Family Therapy). (2005). *Accreditation standards: Graduate & post-graduate marriage and family therapy training programs*. Alexandria, VA: Author.

APA (American Psychological Association). (2009). *Guidelines and principles for accreditation of programs in professional psychology*. Washington, DC: Author.

Aponte, H.J. (1994). How personal can training get? *Journal of Marital and Family Therapy, 20*(1), 3–15.

Aponte, H.J. & Carlsen, C.J. (2009). An instrument for person-of-the-therapist supervision. *Journal of Marital and Family Therapy, 35*, 395–405.

Aponte, H.J. & Winter, J.E. (2013). The person and practice of the therapist: Treatment and training. In M. Baldwin (Ed.), *The use of self in therapy* (3rd ed., pp. 141–165). New York: Routledge.

Aponte, H.J. & Kissil, K. (2014). "If I can grapple with this I can truly be of use in the therapy room": Using the therapist's own emotional struggles to facilitate effective therapy. *Journal of Marital and Family Therapy, 40*(2), 152–164.

Aponte, H.J., Powell, F.D., Brooks, S., Watson, M.F., Litzke, C., Lawless, J. & Johnson, E. (2009). Training the person of the therapist in an academic setting. *Journal of Marital and Family Therapy, 35*, 381–394.

CACREP (Council for Accreditation of Counseling and Related Educational Programs). (2009). *2009 standards*. Alexandria, VA: Author.

COAMFTE (Commission on Accreditation for Marriage and Family Therapy Education). (2013). *Accreditation manual: Policies and procedures*. Alexandria, VA: Author.

CSWE (Counsel on Social Work Education). (2008). *Educational policy and accreditation standards*. Alexandria, VA: Author.

Freshwater, D. (2003). Researching mental health: Pathology in a postmodern world. *Nursing Times Research, 8*(3), 161–172.

Freud, S. (1910). Future prospects of psychoanalytic therapy. In J. Strachey (Ed.), *The standard ed. of the complete works of Sigmund Freud*. (pp. 139–151). London: Hogarth Press.

Garb, H.N. (1989). Clinical judgment, clinical training, and professional experience. *Psychological Bulletin, 105*(3), 387–396.

Garb, H.N. (1994). Social and clinical judgment: Fraught with error? *American Psychologist, 49*(8), 758–759.

Gelman, C.R. (2004). Anxiety experienced by foundation-year MSW students entering field placement: Implications for admissions curriculum, and field education. *Journal of Social Work Education, 40*, 39–54.

Ivey, D.C., Scheel, M.J. & Jankowski, P.J. (1999). A contextual perspective of clinical judgment in couples and family therapy: Is the bridge too far? *Journal of Family Therapy, 21*(4), 339–359.

Jankowski, P.J., Ivey, D.C. & Vaughn, M.J. (2012). Re-visioning a model of clinical judgment for systemic practitioners. *Journal of Systemic Therapies, 31*(3), 17–35.

Kerr, M. & Bowen, M. (1988). *Family evaluation: An approach based on Bowen theory*. New York: WW. Norton.

Lambert, M.J. & Ogles, B.M. (2004). The efficacy and effectiveness of psychotherapy. In M.J. Lambert (Ed.) *Bergin and Garfield's handbook of psychotherapy and behavior change* (5th ed., pp. 139–193). New York: John Wiley and Sons.

Lutz, L. & Irizarry, S.S. (2009). Reflections of two trainees: Person of the therapist training for marriage and family therapists. *Journal of Marital and Family Therapy, 35*, 370–380.

Niño, A., Kissil, K. & Apolinar Claudio, F. (2013). Perceived professional gains of master level students following a person of the therapist training program: A retrospective content analysis. *Journal of Marital and Family Therapy*. Published online October 26. doi: 10.1111/jmft.12051

Nouwen, H.J.M. (1979). *The wounded healer*. New York: Image.

Satir, V. (2013). The therapist story. In M. Baldwin (Ed.), *The use of self in therapy* (3rd ed., pp. 19–27). New York: Routledge.

Smith, T.B., Constantine, M.G., Dunn, T.W., Dinehart, J.M. & Montoya, J.A. (2006). Multicultural education in the mental health professions: A meta-analytic review. *Journal of Counseling Psychology*, *53*(1), 132–145.

Spengler, P.M., White, M.J., Ægisdóttir, S., Maugherman, A.S., Anderson, L.A., Cook, R.S. . . . Rush, J.D. (2009). The meta-analysis of clinical judgment project: Effects of experience on judgment accuracy. *The Counseling Psychologist*, *37*(3), 350–399.

Sprenkle, D.H., Davis, S.D. & Lebow, J.L. (2009). *Common factors in couple and family therapy*. New York: Guilford.

Wampold, B.E. (2010). The research evidence for common factors models: A historically situated perspective. In B.L. Duncan, S.D. Miller, B.E. Wampold, & M.A. Hubble (Eds.), *The heart and soul of change: Delivering what works in therapy* (2nd ed., pp. 49–81). Washington, DC: American Psychological Association.

9 Supervision in the POTT Model

Harry J. Aponte

When supervision in the POTT framework follows a therapist's training in the POTT model on the use of self, there is a natural inclusion of the supervisee's reactions, feelings and life experience in the discussion of the work with the client. Therapists who have not been through a formal training in the POTT model can undergo an abbreviated introductory training experience. This introduction conforms to the core structure of the formal training template (as described in the first few chapters of this book) except that it is conducted between supervisor and supervisee without a group. First, the therapist writes up the presentation of the signature theme—the therapist's idea of the dominant personal issue or issues with which he/she struggles, the history behind the issue and how it may be a problem as well as an asset in doing therapy. The supervisor helps the supervisee develop a clearer conceptualization of the signature theme and its roots, along with possible implications for conducting therapy. The therapist returns with a second write-up that incorporates the insights from the previous meeting, and further refines the thinking. In the third introductory meeting the supervisee writes up a case that will be used to explore in greater depth and detail both how the therapist's issue or issues may be active factors in relating, assessing and intervening with a client, and how the therapist can use his/her life experience (with a special focus on the signature theme) to enhance the effectiveness of his/her work in therapy. Thereafter, supervision will always be conducted around a case, with the therapist's personal issues addressed principally as they relate to the clinical material presented.

The supervisor's task is to help amplify the supervisee's self-awareness within the therapeutic relationship, and guide the therapist to use that self-awareness consciously and purposefully in the therapeutic process. This is done directly in relation to the clinical material. However, the supervisor is also alert to how these same personal issues may appear in the working relationship with the supervisee. The supervisor works with these isomorphic dynamics as they relate to the supervisor/supervisee relationship, and the supervisee/client relationship. The ultimate goal is to help the therapist gain the freedom and ability to use self to give depth of understanding, emotional life and therapeutic effectiveness to the therapeutic process. It may sound and look like therapy at times, and may even be therapeutic, but supervision within the POTT framework is always aimed directly and primarily at enhancing the work with the client.

The Case and the POTT

What follows is a sampling of one such supervisory process with a therapist, here called Martha, who has undergone the POTT training in her graduate program. She was able to engage in supervision directly around her clinical work. Martha articulated her signature theme in these words:

My signature theme revolves around the question of "what is my worth?" In fear that I am worthless and undeserving of love, I over-care (to try to earn worth/value to others); eventually I grow resentful of my own unmet needs and desire to be cared for/made to feel worthy (externally), and withdraw from relationships. Guilt for abandoning others is the surface emotion I then feel; under that is fear of losing the person(s) that help convince me of my worth. In response to the guilt and fear, I then re-engage in over-caring for others.

She related her signature theme to her clinical work in these terms:

I worry that my tendency to self-sacrifice and be the one to fix and control relationships and interactions will make me want to ensure that all my interactions with clients are pleasant or worthwhile for them; I may not want to push topics or allow silences that will make them feel uncomfortable, dislike me, or dislike what I am doing. I worry that my self-sacrificing nature will also lead to quick burn out, as I have already begun investing more time and emotional energy into my clients than is likely healthy. I wonder too if I boost my self-worth by feeling like that special person others confide in, and may depend on this unhealthily in my therapeutic bonds.

Martha's feelings of worthlessness and need of affirmation led her to overextend herself with clients and pressure them to "fix and control relationships and interactions," which I labeled as the need to "perform." Yet, she feared rejection, and so avoided challenging them on hard issues. In the process of pressing for an outcome, she often overrode her own feelings within the therapeutic relationship, as well as those of her clients. As her supervisor, I experienced Martha as bright and talented, quite caring and sensitive. The challenge for me, as her supervisor, was whether I could create an environment in our working relationship that would allow her to be more patient, understanding and accepting of her own human struggles. This self-acceptance would facilitate empathy with her clients through her own personal woundedness, making it possible for her to *be* with her clients as she moved *with* them through their journeys to change. What follows is an example of a supervisory encounter with Martha.

In preparation for our supervisory session, Martha submitted the usual write-up on the case. The following is an abbreviated version of what she prepared.

POTT Supervision Instrument: Case Presentation

1. a. State the agreed upon issue the client is seeking help for in therapy.

Sarah is a 22-year-old woman who came to therapy after being almost 302ed [an involuntary psychiatric hospitalization] for making threats at her former shelter. She wanted to reduce her anger, depression, and anxiety so that she could return to a shelter, stop living with her verbally abusive, crack-addicted mother, and build towards her education and career to make a better life for her daughter.

b. Note anything in it that carries personal meaning for you, including its connections with your signature themes.

She struggles with a lot of loss, is parentified, is a caretaker, felt a lot of loneliness and resentment towards her mom for being emotionally and physically abusive towards her when she was growing up.

2. State the specific topic / concern / question that you want to discuss in today's supervisory session and how it personally touches you.

With Sarah and several other clients with whom I have a really good relationship (ones that I sometimes worry are over-close) I have reduced frequency of contact. I recently reduced to every other week with Sarah due to her real success in treatment, and part of me feels guilty, and picks up on some guardedness from Sarah about that reduction from our weekly sessions. I miss her too.

3. Explain your therapeutic strategy and interventions with the case, and in particular with the aspects of the case you want to discuss in today's supervision.

My work with her has been trauma-focused and emotion-focused. Our early work was on linking her anger to the traumas she has been through from her family and romantic relationships, building compassion and understanding for that anger, and really building a sense of trust and honesty in our relationship.

4. Detail how you could use yourself in conjunction with your interventions. Be specific.

It's been easy for me to intuit her emotions, and sometimes her needs in her relationship with me. I really believe the level of trust we've built has been a contribution to her, and my genuine desire for her to succeed, and belief that she can, has been one of the major mechanisms of change. She has been vulnerable enough to cry and show emotions when I'm correct in my language (she struggles to verbalize, but nods agreement).

5. Please state your current understanding of your signature theme.

I struggle to trust that others can handle themselves and their part in our relationship. As a result I over-assume responsibility, which builds to resentment, which may lead to my distancing. Guilt for abandoning them brings me back to over-caretaking, and the cycle repeats.

During our meeting, I listened to Martha relate how she felt she and Sarah had achieved the major goals of the therapy. Consequently she concluded it "unethical" to keep her client coming on a weekly basis, and felt compelled to perform her duty, that is, to reduce the frequency of visits. She told Sarah she wanted to begin spacing out their sessions from weekly to biweekly. I felt uneasy when she told me this. The decision seemed abrupt and one-sided. Martha had not explored the plan with her client before telling her that they should space out their sessions. She herself was clearly uncomfortable with what she had done, especially after sensing Sarah shutting down emotionally when they talked about the change. However, Martha did not want to base the therapy's planning on her own personal feelings, conscious of the satisfaction she had been enjoying about the progress they had made. She also was aware of a growing attachment to her client, which eventually became apparent as a key issue in reaching her decision about the frequency of sessions with Sarah and how she handled how she communicated it to her.

The Person of the Supervisor

As we talked about this last encounter with Sarah, a clinical incident of my own spontaneously came to mind. I recalled a session with a client-family years before. In the middle of that session I had suddenly found I was blank, not knowing where to go next. There was nothing to grab onto, no door to even knock on. I was accustomed to identifying goals with clients, mobilizing all the energy in the room to systematically pursue them. The feeling I now vividly connected to was not only the sense of helplessness I had felt at that moment, but also how I had decided not to fight it. I chose to stop pressing, and be present in the moment, which meant being conscious, aware of the family and of myself at that very moment. I paid particular attention to whatever thoughts and feelings were spontaneously coming up for me. I do not now recall the words or the content, just trying to let go, and talking with them about them— getting more of a feeling about them. I stopped pressing, then suddenly a strong intuition crystalized for me about what was driving the issues we had been discussing. I risked a guess, and shared it with them. A door opened, and we were soon into the heart of their struggle, and the session took off.

That one experience with that family changed my therapy. Much in my life had conditioned me to press the therapeutic process toward an outcome, much as Martha tended to do. I had grown up working hard to make things happen in my life. My parents were migrants to the U.S., I was born here, but we did not speak English at home, our means were limited, and they could do little to help me with the world outside. Home was also a troubled family environment, and I felt compelled from early life to take control and manage life by myself. However, I also had a place in me where I could access an active quietude. I had attended a parochial school where I learned a spirituality in which paradoxically while taking responsibility for our personal and moral choices, we were also conscious of the limits on our control over life. The ultimate control was elsewhere. It helped with letting go of the need to control. So in that session I revisited the "letting go" that I knew from back then, and it released my intuition from the pressure to act. These experiences and knowledge that came up for me while talking with Martha about her client clarified for me that I had to help Martha do the same in her relationship with her client.

And so now with Martha, I attended to the discomfort I felt when she said she told her client they could start meeting biweekly instead of weekly. I experienced a fleeting sense of abandonment, and wondered how the client had reacted. Martha had told me that the client's issues were tied to a distrust of relationships because of the neglect and abandonment she experienced in her family, but that she had come to experience a degree of real trust in her. In response to my query about how she was feeling about what happened between her and Sarah, Martha admitted feeling a sense of loss because she had become attached to the client, having identified with her because of her own experience of emotional aloneness. Throughout her childhood her mother was too incapacitated with cancer to care for her, and her father too impaired because of his alcoholism to be of help to her. She had learned early in life to deny her own needs in order to care for her family, much like Sarah had learned to shut down to her own need for care and attention because her parents were too preoccupied with their problems to be there for her. After we put this all together, Martha realized she had to dial back the clock and restart the weekly sessions with her client.

Martha and I were able to trace her duty-over-feeling decision to her childhood denial of her own personal needs to meet her duties as a juvenile caregiver. My own access to a resonant past experience of my own facilitated my fostering Martha's fuller understanding of herself to rethink the troublesome intervention with her client.

After the supervisory session, I received the customary Post-Supervisory Questionnaire, abbreviated here, which we discussed at our next meeting.

Post-Supervisory Questionnaire

1. Was your thinking and feeling about yourself and/or the way you relate to others affected by the discussion in the supervisory session? If so, how?

I hadn't noted my need "to perform" ["fix and control"] before this session, but see it in almost all of my [therapeutic] relationships now.

2. Did the discussion in the supervisory session help you to increase your understanding of your signature(s) theme(s)? If so, how?

Somewhat, by adding the above piece. It left me feeling emotionally confused though, and a little more wary of trusting myself [with] others.

3. How can you connect what you have presented in the previous two questions with your clinical work?

If I spend so much time performing in anticipation of what my clients may need, I won't be able to, a) connect to see what they do need, b) self-reflect and see what I can give, and what

I can't, c) then communicate that to them in a way that creates understanding of human and relationship limitations.

Martha recognizes that "performing" has been overriding her "feelings," that is, that her actions are being largely directed by her head at the expense of her heart. This leads to her not trusting herself with "others," i.e. her clients, because it also results in her overriding her perceptions of their feelings. She comes to the unsettling realization that this is happening in almost all her therapeutic relationships. She is now intent on changing, but she will need some help along the way.

In a follow-up communication Martha reported:

I called her up and set back up weekly appointments with her. She asked why; I stated I felt I had reduced our sessions abruptly without seeking her input, and that I wanted to resume weekly sessions until we both agreed it was time to reduce. She agreed to come weekly. When I see her next week I want to tell her I also felt distancing from her, wondered if my reduction felt hurtful, and ask what my reduction in sessions felt like for her. I feel way better with the idea of acknowledging what I feel happening with my client/in the room/in our relationship, rather than avoiding it out of guilt or fear that another can't state their feelings or needs.

In our following meeting she was anxious about her next session with this client. She wanted to plan how to deal with the client's anger about abandonment. However, she was hearing from me to prioritize being fully present with her client so she could better engage with her mutually in their relationship process before trying to *do* anything. Martha was torn between taking control of the session to solve the problem with her client and the idea of *sharing* control of the work with the client, something that made her anxious.

We also had the isomorphic experience in her relationship with me, as her supervisor. She got in touch with how her relationship with me was no exception, and that she unconsciously tended to exercise control in our working relationship. She had come to realize that she was working so hard to meet what she thought were my expectations that she was out of touch with deeper needs of her own that she had in our process. In particular she was not claiming time to speak about her feelings of shame, guilt and failure for not doing a better job in her therapy. She was too concerned that I would be disappointed in her performance. All this threw her back to her relationship with her parents, especially with her father. She had been solicitous when he was drinking most heavily during his wife's illness, but also leaned emotionally on him during the latter period of his life when he was struggling to be sober and Martha felt closest to him. She had to be in control in that relationship to care for him, even as she sought his approval of how good a daughter she was being. We agreed that we would more consciously work to make our supervisory process a place where she could feel freer to speak to her vulnerabilities. It was for me to help create a supervisory relationship where she felt safe to be a struggling therapist—something I could relate to as a therapist who at one time also struggled to have it all too much under his control.

Following our supervisory session she wrote (here abbreviated):

Post-Supervisory Questionnaires

Post-Supervisory Questionnaire for POTT Issues Discussions

1. Was your thinking and feeling about yourself and/or the way you relate to others affected by the discussion in the supervisory session? If so, how?
My tendency (and desire) to control relationships to keep me safe (and generally distant) was made very clear for me again.

2. Did the discussion in the supervisory session help you to increase your understanding of your signature(s) theme(s)? If so, how?
Same as above.

3. How can you connect what you have presented in the previous two questions with your clinical work?
I really hope that by learning how to have a mutual relationship in our supervision, and starting to honor and communicate my needs as a priority, that I will learn to create and model the same for my clients. I believe more strongly in that idea, and feel motivated to learn this art.

As our supervisory work evolved, we touched on other layers of what she was dealing with within herself that had potent connections to her work with her clients. She highlighted another component of her signature theme, which spoke not as much about her need to be seen as performing competently as it did about her fear of being hurt and let down if she allowed herself to depend on others—something she could not do in her childhood with her parents. For her to work in partnership with her supervisor, she would need to have access and give expression to the struggle within herself about being dependent on her supervisor. She recently experienced how this translated in her work with clients. Her own client had shut herself down emotionally to avoid being further disappointed by her therapist. Martha was personally challenged to regain her client's trust. In the process, she would be helping her client learn what she herself was trying to learn—the way a healthy dependency can discern how and under what circumstances to depend on another person while remaining grounded within one's self.

In our last supervisory session around the featured case we again went into talking about how she herself grew up feeling responsible for tuning into and being helpful to her seriously ill mother and alcoholic father. While she was rewarded with appreciation from both parents, she did not feel taken care of by them emotionally. She invests in relationships, but holds herself back emotionally for fear of being disappointed by the other person, who like her parents may not be able to give her the kind of consideration and care she needs in the relationship. In her professional relationships she feels responsible for the recovery or healing of her clients, which eventually may feel so burdensome to her that she may shut down emotionally in the relationships.

On the other hand, Martha recognizes that she functions as if the person on the other side of the relationship is not going to take her into account, and so consequently she does not tap into her own needs and sensitivities in the give and take of the relationship. This inhibits her ability to read the impact of her client's behavior on her, which denies her the information she might cull from her own reactions to clients—information that can tell her something about the client in an aspect of the interaction that is not being communicated through words. Moreover, not fully attending to how clients may feel or react to her does not allow for a full consciousness of the mutuality in the therapeutic relationship. Her greater awareness of the personal reactions of both her and her clients in their interactions with each other will help her make more room not only for her own consciousness about what drives her in those interactions, but also for her clients' emotions and needs, which facilitates their being more self-driven in their transactions with her, making for greater mutuality in their therapeutic process.

The issue needed to be simultaneously addressed in the supervisory relationship, where she was working hard to be a "good supervisee" but was not putting forth all of her needs and expectations. The isomorphic dynamics of all this were quite apparent.

Further into the Process

Further down the road of our supervisory work she gave feedback on a supervisory session we had on another case similar to the one we followed above. We see here the progression of Martha's insights into her own inner workings and their reflection in her clinical work.

Post-Supervisory Questionnaires (abbreviated)

Post-Supervisory Questionnaire for POTT Issues Discussions

1. Was your thinking and feeling about yourself and/or the way you relate to others affected by the discussion in the supervisory session? If so, how?

Yes. I am starting to see more clearly now how harmful my over-caretaking, and subsequent cut off is for others, in that they end up losing me (even worse after I've worked extra hard to give what I think they want). I've been struck by how rarely, also, I feel deserving of others' wanting to connect with me, and the ways I try to make up for my belief that they do not want to connect with me (over-caring, over-scheduling social time, over-scheduling clients).

2. Did the discussion in the supervisory session help you to increase your understanding of your signature(s) theme(s)? If so, how?

I'm seeing the impact on others more now. I'm also currently feeling more trapped by these themes than before (with an over-full client schedule that I know I need to change but am afraid of losing or hurting people, or maybe of not being missed or wanted).

3. How can you connect what you have presented in the previous two questions with your clinical work?

I'm hurting the client I spoke about by making her over-dependent on me, then cutting her off abruptly (I said today she could call even if not suicidal, but also set a boundary [that felt softer] by letting her know my time may be limited, but that I will call her back; I just need to keep this softer boundary, and see myself as deserving of my own needs and self-care too).

4. How my use of self with this case was influenced.

In session today I partnered a lot more with her, not over-assuming responsibility, but asking her what she needed right now. I noticed anxiety about not DOING something when she was in real distress, but was able to focus more on being with her where she was. She still ended up calling out of work, but I know I would have felt more frustration and disappointment (I still felt a twinge of it, which is probably part of why I'm exhausted now) if I had over-invested the way I normally do.

5. Questions that remain about my conduct of this case.

She ended up reaching out to her mom, explaining some attachment ruptures, and feeling heard. She is considering a family session. I'm unclear how I would structure that, but want to help reinforce her attachments elsewhere, while not completely cutting the attachment with me (though I'm already feeling worn out by over-working for her).

We can see here changes in her efforts to balance client-care with self-care. We witness her self-awareness and sensitivity to attachments between self and client, and client with other family. We also get a glimpse into how she is applying her insights about her clinical work to a broad spectrum of areas in her personal life. While I am focused on her gaining personal self-awareness that relates to her clinical work, Martha is applying what she is learning about herself to the rest of her life. Changes are taking place both in her clinical work and personal life. Each affects the other.

A Caution

Self-awareness and self-monitoring in our clinical relationships will inevitably reflect back on our personal lives. The supervisor takes from supervisees' personal lives to help them improve clinical performance, and the supervisees take from their clinical insights to better their personal lives. There is a careful line to be walked in this personal/professional process of supervision (Aponte, 1994). The supervisor promotes self-awareness in the supervisee so the supervisee can monitor self in the therapeutic process, utilizing that self-awareness to maximize his/her own effectiveness in the relationship, to read the client through his/herself in assessing the client and the client's issue, and in implementing an intervention most effectively through the connection with the client. In the POTT model, this personal self-awareness is linked directly to the therapist's clinical performance. However, as seen in the supervisory example here cited, supervisees will draw implications from these self-insights about their personal life experiences in ways that will often move them to strive to make changes in their personal lives. Such efforts to make personal changes corresponding to the personal changes made in clinical self-management may well facilitate their efforts to change how they use themselves in their therapeutic relationships, something any supervisor would welcome. However, here is the caution. Supervisors are also therapists, of course, and the temptation to commit to fostering these personal changes in their supervisees' personal lives can be seductive. The problem, of course, is that if the supervisory process that can be therapeutic becomes therapy, the supervisor's focus on clinical oversight becomes diluted by the concern for the supervisee's personal goals. We are left with poor supervision and poor therapy, along with the potential of violating professional and ethical standards (AAMFT, Code of Ethics).

There are five guidelines that a supervisor working within the POTT model may observe to stay within the boundaries of the supervisory responsibility:

1. Prioritize for yourself in supervision clarity about the clinical objectives of the cases you are discussing.
2. Always conclude any discussion of supervisees' personal issues with their connection to the supervisees' clinical material.
3. Monitor your own personal investment in supervisees' personal growth and change so as to remain clearly within the boundaries of your commitment to supervisees' clinical responsibilities and effectiveness.
4. Do not hesitate to look for supervision or consultation of your supervision when you find yourself becoming too personally concerned about supervisees' personal life issues.
5. Be prepared to suggest and/or refer supervisees to therapy with external resources when appropriate.

Finally, let us not forget that there is a person of the supervisor. We have our own personal issues that will impact how we supervise. We should be as personally self-aware in our supervisory roles as we expect our supervisees should be in their therapeutic roles. In this process we, the supervisors, have a chance to learn from our experience supervising what will benefit our own personal lives. To the extent that we work, perhaps with help, on making our personal life experience enrich our work as supervisors, we will enhance our skills in helping our supervisees in the use of their personal selves in the therapy they do.

References

AAMFT (American Association for Marriage and Family Therapy), Code of Ethics (Effective July 1, 2012). Principle 1.3, Multiple Relationships. Web site: www.aamft. org/iMIS15/AAMFT/Content/legal_ethics/code_of_ethics.aspx

Aponte, H.J. (1994). How personal can training get? *Journal of Marital and Family Therapy, 20*(1), 3–15.

Appendix A
Fall Quarter Materials

1. POTT SYLLABUS: FALL QUARTER (ABBREVIATED)

Course Description

The POTT course will enable students to make fuller use of themselves in the practice of therapy. Students will develop insight into their own personal life experiences (emotional, socio-cultural and spiritual), with particular emphasis on their personal life struggles (signature themes). Through lecture, class presentations and clinical experiences, they will learn how to use these insights proactively to better relate to their clients and more effectively use themselves in addressing their clients' issues.

Expanded Course Description

Most self-of-the-therapist approaches to training and supervision view *resolution* of personal issues as a necessary means of change and growth that frees therapists to become more effective professionals. Nevertheless, our clients get who we are *in the present*, not who we would like to be. The POTT approach emphasizes learning the intentional use of self *as-is*. The POTT model adopts the concept of the "wounded healer." It is through our woundedness that we can empathize with and relate to the woundedness of others. Further, our wounds can be powerful tools allowing us to feel our clients' pain, understand their life struggles and speak to their will to change. By promoting awareness and acceptance of ourselves and our own struggles, POTT helps therapists understand how these issues can affect their therapeutic work. Most importantly, this approach promotes the intentional use of who we are, with our strengths and shortcomings, for the purpose of enhancing our clinical effectiveness. Through lecture, class presentations and clinical experiences, students will learn to use these insights proactively to better relate to their clients and more effectively use themselves in addressing their clients' issues.

Course Objectives

Students will use the POTT training to learn how to work with and through their personal selves in their therapeutic roles. The course aims for three basic objectives.

Students will:

1. Gain an understanding of themselves, particularly about the aspects of their humanity that will enable them to relate to the woundedness of their clients.
2. Grow in the ability to access the aspects of themselves (emotional, socio-cultural and spiritual) that potentially enhance the effectiveness of their work with clients.
3. Develop the ability to use themselves consciously and purposefully in the effective practice of their craft.

Course Learning Outcomes

Students who successfully complete this course will be able to:

1. Identify core emotional issues (signature themes) that affect their personal lives, and potentially affect their clinical work.
2. Identify specific ways in which these core issues potentially affect their clinical practice with respect to their relationship with clients, their assessment of clients and their interventions with clients.
3. Recognize in practice how these issues are triggered by and relate to their therapeutic process with clients (the relationship, assessment and interventions) in vivo, as they actually engage with the client in therapy.
4. Develop specific skills to use these issues of theirs along with their life experience and worldview in positive, proactive ways in their therapy.
5. Identify how to incorporate these use-of-self skills into the therapeutic model of their choice.

Required Readings

Aponte, H.J. (2009). Introduction for special section on training and supervision. *Journal of Marital and Family Therapy*, *35*, 369.

Aponte, H.J. & Carlsen, C.J. (2009). An instrument for person-of-the-therapist supervision. *Journal of Marital and Family Therapy*, *35*, 395–405.

Aponte, H.J. & Kissil, K. (2014). "If I can grapple with this I can truly be of use in the therapy room": Using the therapist's own emotional struggles to facilitate effective therapy. *Journal of Marital and Family Therapy*, *40*, 152–164.

Aponte, H.J., Powell, F.D., Brooks, S., Watson, M.F., Litzke, C., Lawless, J. & Johnson, E. (2009). Training the person of the therapist in an academic setting. *Journal of Marital and Family Therapy*, *35*, 381–394.

Lutz, L. & Irizarry, S.S. (2009). Reflections of two trainees: Person of the therapist training for marriage and family therapists. *Journal of Marital and Family Therapy*, *35*, 370–380.

Recommended Texts

Baldwin, M. (Ed.). (2013). *The use of self in therapy* (3rd ed.). New York: Routledge.

McGoldrick, M., Shellenberger, S. & Petry, S. (2008). *Genograms: Assessment and intervention* (3rd ed.). New York, NY: Norton.

Method of Instruction

The method of instruction will consist of lectures, student presentations on their personal selves as related to their clinical practice and case presentations with emphasis on how personal factors play out in the way the students relate, assess and intervene with their clients.

Course Requirements

Summary of Readings and Questions

For weeks following reading assignments, please come prepared with a brief paragraph and question/thought (for each reading). Hard copies of your reading assignment write-ups will be collected in class.

Signature Theme Presentations I and II

Starting on the fourth week of classes, every week two students will make their presentations. The instructions for the signature theme presentations I and II will be posted. **You must follow these outlines**. Your written presentation should be emailed to your professor and teaching assistant by *Monday at NOON of the week you are scheduled to present*. These written presentations are worth 15 percent of the final grade. It is imperative that the trainers have ample opportunity to review your material prior to the presentation in order to maximize the use of time, and, if necessary, consult with you prior to the presentation.

- **Signature theme presentation (first presentation)**: In this presentation you will introduce your signature theme, locate it in your personal and/or family history and discuss how this could manifest in your clinical work. See posted outline.
- **Expanded signature theme presentation (second presentation)**: in this presentation you will expand on your signature theme based on the feedback you have received from your first presentation. Make sure to reflect on the feedback received and incorporate it into your presentation. This presentation is not a repeat of your first presentation; instead it is an opportunity to build on your past presentation.

These presentations will be videotaped. It is expected that the students use these videos to inform the write-up of their final papers.

Final Paper

In this paper you will describe how your understanding of your signature theme, its origins and its clinical implications have evolved following your signature theme presentations, and how you related these insights to a particular case. Instructions for the final paper will be posted. **You must follow this outline**. This paper is 50 percent of the final grade.

Journals

Students are required to journal every week, as soon as possible after the end of class, when the reactions to and memories of the class presentations are still fresh. In each journal, the students will address the following:

1. What did you experience during your classmate's presentation? What feelings and thoughts came up for you? What resonated for you? What could you relate to?
2. How did this presentation relate to your signature theme and your clinical work?

[Note: Journal writing assignments will begin following the first class.]

You can either follow this format if you find it helpful, or you can write your own narrative about your experiences during class. To benefit most from this assignment, challenge yourself to be open and vulnerable. Remember that the focus of attention is not what others presented but your personal insights about it, and how you link those to your signature theme. The purpose of the journal is to help you to actively engage in self-reflection. We encourage you to take advantage of the feedback you receive in your journals each week and incorporate it in your work. The deadline for submission is <u>Monday at noon</u>. Each journal is worth five points.

Outline of Course Assignments and Readings

Class 1: Introduction and Orientation to the POTT Training

Class 2: From each of the JMFT articles (not the Introduction), please come prepared with a brief paragraph and question/ thought (for each reading).

Hard copies of your reading assignment write-ups will be collected in class.

Aponte, H.J. (2009). Introduction for special section on training and supervision. *Journal of Marital and Family Therapy*, *35*, 369.

Aponte, H.J. & Kissil, K. (2014). "If I can grapple with this I can truly be of use in the therapy room": Using the therapist's own emotional struggles to facilitate effective therapy. *Journal of Marital and Family Therapy*, *40*, 152–164.

Aponte, H.J., Powell, F.D., Brooks, S., Watson, M.F., Litzke, C., Lawless, J. & Johnson, E. (2009). Training the person of the therapist in an academic setting. *Journal of Marital and Family Therapy*, *35*, 381–394.

Class 3: From each of the JMFT articles please come prepared with a brief paragraph and question/thought (for each reading).

Hard copies of your reading assignment write-ups will be collected in class.

Aponte, H.J. & Carlsen, C.J. (2009). An instrument for person-of-the-therapist supervision. *Journal of Marital and Family Therapy, 35,* 395–405.

Lutz, L. & Irizarry, S.S. (2009). Reflections of two trainees: Person of the therapist training for marriage and family therapists. *Journal of Marital and Family Therapy, 35,* 370–380.

Niño, A., Kissil, K. & Apolinar Claudio, F. (2013). (published on-line 10/26/13). Perceived professional gains of master level students following a person of the therapist training program: A retrospective content analysis. *Journal of Marital and Family Therapy.* doi: 10.1111/jmft.12051

Signature theme presentations: From Class 4 to Class 10, two students per class will present on their signature themes.

2. CONFIDENTIALITY STATEMENT

An important distinction can be made between students' signature themes and their personal histories. On the one hand, personal signature themes are core issues that students will need to address openly with trainers and supervisors to the extent they affect their work with clients. On the other hand, their personal histories, which are tied to their genograms and explored in the POTT classes, need not be shared in other parts of the program.

Students are asked to keep what they learn about each other in the POTT class among themselves, and to speak to such personal information outside the POTT class only to the extent that the individual being referenced is present and invites the conversation. The only exception to this agreement occurs when students journal on the impact of other students' personal information on them as part of their personal reflections in their confidential class journals. Students are told not to feel obligated to reveal personal history in other classes, or in group or individual supervision. Moreover, it is made clear to them that in all circumstances what they decide to reveal about themselves to faculty and other students is strictly their choice. Students are made aware that the personal material they share in their POTT presentations is not kept confidential from faculty who have a responsibility to make judgments about their professional development. However, school faculty does not share students' personal histories from their POTT classes with field supervisors or anyone else in their field placements.

Signature: _____

Name: _____

Date: _____

3. OUTLINE FOR SIGNATURE THEME PRESENTATION AND PAPER

Your Signature Theme

Describe what you believe to be the personal issue that has been most dominant in your life. This is the hang-up of yours that has and continues to vex you, affecting many or all areas of your life. Take into consideration the emotional, spiritual and social components of your life.

Your Struggle with Your Signature Theme

Speak to how you deal with your signature theme. Here describe where you handle it poorly, and where you deal with it most effectively. Add who in your life is most helpful to you in wrestling with it, and how you make good use of this person's help.

Your Genogram

Attach a three generational genogram of your family, with comments that may help us understand who the characters are and their relationships to one another.

Your Family History

Provide a history of your family, as you believe it relates to your signature theme. These are your hypotheses about the parts your family members and their relationships may have contributed to the origin and perpetuation of your signature theme.

Your Clinical Work

Offer your thoughts on how you believe your signature theme has affected or may affect your relationship with clients and your work with their issues—negatively and positively.

Appendix B
Winter Quarter Materials

1. POTT SYLLABUS: WINTER QUARTER (EXTRACT)

Course Requirements

Case Presentations

Starting on the third week of classes, two students will make their presentations every week. The instructions for case presentations are below and also posted. **You must follow these outlines**. Your written presentation and client genogram should be emailed to your professors by ***Monday at NOON of the week you are scheduled to present***. This written presentation is worth 15 percent of the grade. It is imperative that the trainers have ample opportunity to review your material prior to the presentation in order to maximize the use of time and if necessary consult with you prior to the presentation. *Late submissions will not be eligible for full credit. Papers that are submitted a week after the deadline will not be accepted, and the student will receive no credit for the assignment.*

Case Presentations Outline

First Presentation

FORMAT: Your paper may be up to seven (7) pages long. It must be typed, double-spaced and include a cover page. In addition, please proofread and spell-check your document prior to submission. Papers with grammatical errors, etc., will not be eligible for full credit.

AIM: Your task in this written assignment is to demonstrate how you apply what you learned about your signature theme via your presentation into your relationship(s) and clinical work with clients. This first presentation focuses on how aware you are of the areas below.

Areas to include:

1. Your Signature Theme: Clearly identify your signature theme and describe how your understanding of your signature theme has evolved following your presentation and participation in the POTT experience.
2. Your Clinical Work: In the first presentation, you shared your thoughts about how your signature theme might affect your clinical work. In the final paper, you are required to provide a case example and show how your signature theme and other personal characteristics of your life came up in your relationship and work with a specific client.

Identifying information regarding the client:

*   Genogram of client.
*   Agreed upon issue the client is seeking help for and personal meaning for you.
*   Personal reactions to the client and vice versa.
*   Cultural or spiritual values that possibly inform your view of the issues.
*   Hypotheses about the root(s) and dynamics of the client's issue(s).
*   Personal challenges in relating and working with the client around their issue(s).
*   Concrete plan for meeting your personal challenges in the case.

Second Presentation

For the second presentation students' write-ups will follow the format of the first presentation. However, they are expected to incorporate the insights they gained from their first presentation about how aspects of their signature themes and life experiences may influence a clinical encounter. In class they will demonstrate what they learned through a video clip of an actual clinical session or through a role-play of a clinical session. In other words, students are presenting on how their personal selves may adversely affect their clinical performance, as well as how they can purposefully use their signature themes and personal live experiences positively to connect, assess and intervene with clients in the therapeutic process.

[Note for Students: In both presentations, you will describe a clinical case, show a video of your work with these clients and reflect on how your signature theme and other person-of-the-therapist factors are playing out in your work. For this presentation, students are expected to obtain videotapes of their clinical work. This process should be no different than acquiring a release for super-vision. The student is responsible for obtaining a release to videotape, and reviewing the purposes of videotaping (i.e. training and supervision) with all clients. You should note whether or not your practicum site's release of information makes reference to disclosure for training purposes. If your release of information does not contain this information, please discuss this with your on-site supervisor and the Director of Clinical Training Programs.]

These presentations will be videotaped. It is expected that the students use these videos to inform the write-up of their final papers. *Make sure videos are ready to be played BEFORE your presentation and check the amount of room on camera memory cards.*

[Notes: All submitted presentation documents will be emailed to the class before each presentation date.

CLIENT CONFIDENTIALITY: Do not use identifying information in case presentation papers (use pseudonyms and leave out places of work, school, etc.). DELETE or SHRED all papers following presentations to protect clients' confidentiality.]

Final Paper

Your final case presentation paper involves elaboration and refinement of your rough draft. Your presentation experience will enable you to integrate specific feedback into the paper. The POTT process is different for everyone; therefore, the steps you take writing your final papers will be unique. ***The outline for the final paper is the same as for the presentation paper (rough draft). You must follow this outline.***

This paper is 50 percent of the final grade. The final paper is due on the last day class in the winter quarter. If you are presenting on a Friday, your final paper will be due the following **Monday at noon**. For the final deadline, the paper *should be emailed to all instructors before the last class has ended (paper copies are not necessary).* Late submissions will not be accepted and students who do not turn their paper in on time will not receive credit for the assignment.

Important notes about clinical case presentations and papers:

- **Plan to present 15–20 minutes of your video in class. For the first presentation show a segment in which you are aware of how you are using yourself in therapy. For the second presentation show a segment in which you are purposefully attempting to use yourself in therapy, based upon your awareness of your signature theme(s).**
- Use of video is strongly recommended as it will best prepare you to examine yourself for developmental purposes.
- It is strongly recommended that students consider presenting the SAME CASE for both presentations. Although this is not mandatory, it can provide a deeper clinical understanding of POTT issues.
- ***The final paper for the case presentation only needs to be based on one case****. If you presented on two different cases, choose one to use as your final paper. If you presented twice on one case, combine write-ups for your final paper.*

- Please see outline for writing case presentations (will be posted). Also, consult the syllabus for further guidance about writing these papers.

Outline of Course Assignments and Readings

Class 1: Class topic: The self in the therapeutic relationship, clinical assessment and technical intervention (lecture)

Class 2: Class topic: Dr. Aponte's video (lecture and discussion)

Class 3: Two presentations

Class 4: Two presentations

Class 5: Two presentations

Class 6: Two presentations

Class 7: Two presentations

Class 8: Two presentations

Class 9: Two presentations

Class 10: Two presentations

2. CLINICAL CASE PRESENTATION AND PAPER GUIDE

FORMAT: Your paper may be up to seven (7) pages long. It must be typed, double-spaced and include a cover page. In addition, please proofread and spell-check your document prior to submission. Papers with grammatical errors, etc., will not be eligible for full credit.

AIM: Your task in this written assignment is to recognize how what you bring of your personal self to the clinical process affects the work you are doing with clients, in particular, with respect to your relationship, assessment and interventions in the therapeutic encounter.

Areas to include:

1. Your Signature Theme: Clearly identify your signature theme and describe how your understanding of your signature theme has evolved following your presentations and participation in the POTT experience.
2. Your Clinical Work: In the first presentation, you sought to identify and understand your signature theme, and how it might affect your clinical work. In this presentation, you provide a case example and show how your signature theme came up in your relationship and work with a specific client. We ask that, if possible, you present in class a 10–15 minute video that illustrates the points you want to focus on in your presentation.

The paper should be structured according to the following outline:

- My signature theme as I understand it today.
- Identifying information regarding the client, and context of the clinical process.
- Genogram of client.
- Agreed upon issue the client is seeking help for and personal meaning for you.
- Personal reactions to the client and vice versa.
- Cultural or spiritual values that possibly inform your view of the issues.
- Hypotheses about the root(s) and dynamics of the clients' issue(s).
- Personal challenges in relating and working with the client around their issue(s).
- Your observations and analysis about how what you brought personally to the therapeutic process, and the signature theme in particular, affected your relationship and work with your client.

3. ROLE-PLAY OPTIONS

Students have the option of engaging in a role-play of a clinical session for one of their two clinical presentations. They can choose between two formats for the role-plays in which the students will be supervised live in how to observe, reflect on what is happening in the moment in the therapeutic process and how they plan to use themselves in relating, assessing and intervening. The clients will be portrayed by other students from the class.

1. The clients are walk-ins, and the student therapist conducts an initial interview with the goals of connecting therapeutically, identifying the focal issue, and developing hypotheses for the dynamics underlying the issue with the final goal of attaining a commitment to treatment from the clients.
2. The clients represent an actual case they are working on.

Appendix C
Spring Quarter Materials

1. POTT SYLLABUS: SPRING QUARTER (EXTRACT)

Course Requirements

Simlab Experience

Each student will be required to participate once in simulation lab (simlab), over the course of the term. Each student will sign up ahead of time for an assigned slot. There will be one simulated clinical experience each week (lasting 45 minutes) where each student will work with a simulated case performed by trained actors. Actors will depict a couple or family and a broad outline of a scenario will have been preplanned, but the issues and relationships will evolve from class to class with each new student therapist. Each student will be expected to be conscious of how their signature theme is being triggered by the family and its issues, and of how they can use it to further therapeutic goals. Each student will be supervised conducting a 45-minute session with a simulated client family or couple. Meanwhile, the rest of the class will observe the session. The second part of the class will involve discussing the experience.

Important Considerations

Presentations will be videotaped and accessible via the Orion system associated with simlab. All students should use these videos to inform the write-up of their final papers. Individual cameras will be used to record the discussion after the simlab presentation. *Make sure videos are ready to be played BEFORE your presentation and check the amount of room on camera memory cards.*

---

2. SIMLAB FEEDBACK: QUESTIONS FOR THE THERAPIST

After the session with the simulated clients, the actors will provide feedback to the students following this guideline:

Questions about the person of the therapist	*Feedback on building the relationship*	*Feedback on assessment*	*Feedback on intervention*	*What questions do you have for us?*
What did you most like about working with us?	What we liked most about how you related to us	What made us feel most understood by you	What we found most helpful about your work with us	
What did you find most challenging about working with us?	What we liked least about how you related with us	What made us feel least understood by you	What we found least helpful about your work with us	

3. SIMLAB PAPER AND PAPER GUIDE

In this paper, you will describe your work with the family, relating the role your signature theme played in your work in several areas: your connection with your clients, your assessment of the case and your interventions. The instructions for simlab presentations will be posted. **Students are required to adhere to these outlines, or they risk not receiving credit for the assignment**. Final student write-ups are due at the beginning of the ***last day of class***. This written presentation is worth 65 percent of the grade.

Important notes about simlab presentations and papers:

- Please see outline for writing simlab papers (will be posted), consult the syllabus for further guidance (see rubrics below).
- This will be a simulated therapy experience where Dr. Aponte and your co-instructor provide you with live feedback and guidance as you work with client-actors. This is not a test; it is an opportunity to receive POTT feedback. You will receive feedback via an earpiece and will be asked to step out of the therapy room several times throughout the session to talk to your professors about your process.
- There is nothing you need to do to prepare for the simlab experience. **Please make sure to bring your video cameras to record the post-session discussion.** We recommend focusing on being present and connected to your clients during the simulated session.
- As aforementioned, there will not be a rough draft for the simlab paper. Although the paper will be due at the end of the quarter, we recommend writing it as soon as possible after your presentation day. We will be available should you have questions. Your video recording will be helpful to you in your writing process.
- Please make sure to check the schedule for presentations (will be posted).

Simlab Paper Guide

About the therapist:

Signature theme: Briefly state your present understanding of your signature theme.

About the case:

1. Clients' general information (ages, gender, relationships, occupation, etc.).
2. Case genogram.
3. Clients' focal issue.
4. Hypothesis about the focal issue (historical roots and current underlying dynamics that maintain the problem).
5. What are the clients' social locations, and how did they affect your relationship with the clients and your work with them?
6. Therapeutic strategy and approach.

About the person of the therapist with this particular case— therapeutic use of self.

1. What was triggered for you personally (emotionally and/or values-wise) in this session in the relationship with the clients? In dealing with the clients' issues?

Here is where you identify what you are personally experiencing in your interactions with your clients, particularly as related to your signature theme.

2. What did you draw from your own personal life experience and worldview in this session in relating to your clients? In dealing with their issues?

Here is where you describe how you made use of yourself and your inner process to empathize and connect with your clients, to both identify with and differentiate from them, and to actively and purposefully assess and intervene.

3. How did this case challenge you in relating, assessing and/or intervening with your clients, and how did you deal with the challenge?

Paper writing: The paper should be four to six pages in length, double-spaced, with a 12-point font, following the APA format. Please include appropriate headings in your writing.

This is not a research paper. So, no references are required, but if outside sources are used, please cite and reference the source as per APA guidelines.

4. FINAL REFLECTION PAPER GUIDE

Please respond to the following questions in relation to three areas: personal change, professional growth and class process. Use a separate page for each question.

Personal change: Reflecting on the process you went through this year, how has the view of your signature theme changed? What personal changes have taken place in you and in your relationships as a result of the experiences that you had in this class? (Remember to share only what you would like to make known to your instructors. You need not share any personal information.)

Professional growth: Reflecting on the process you went through this year, how has your clinical practice and your perception of yourself as a therapist changed as a result of the experiences that you had in this class? How do you see your clinical skills improving with respect to relationship with clients, assessment and intervention?

Feedback about the class: What about the class was helpful for you in your process? What would you have wanted to be different in the class?

Appendix D

Supervisory Materials
(For supervisees formally trained
in the POTT model)

1. POTT SUPERVISION INSTRUMENT: CASE PRESENTATION

Supervisee: _____
Date of supervision: _____

1. a. State the agreed upon issue the client is seeking help for in therapy.
   b. Note anything in it that carries personal meaning for you, including its connections with your signature themes.
2. State the specific topic/concern/question that you want to discuss in today's supervisory session and how it personally touches you.
3. State your particular hypothesis of the core issues of the client, and how those are playing out in different areas.
4. Explain your therapeutic strategy and interventions with the case, and in particular with the aspects of the case you want to discuss in today's supervision.
5. Detail how you could use yourself in conjunction with your interventions. Be specific.
6. State your current level of understanding of your signature themes.

2. POST-SUPERVISORY QUESTIONNAIRES

Supervisee: _____

Date of supervision: _____

Post-Supervisory Questionnaire for <u>POTT</u> <u>Issues Discussions</u>

1. Was your thinking and feeling about yourself and/or the way you relate to others affected by the discussion in the supervisory session? If so, how?
2. Did the discussion in the supervisory session help you to increase your understanding of your signature(s) theme(s)? If so, how?
3. How can you connect what you have presented in the previous two questions with your clinical work?
4. Please state your current understanding of your signature theme.

Post-Supervisory Questionnaire for <u>Case Presentations</u>

1. How my thinking and feelings about this case were changed.
2. How my therapeutic strategy with this case was influenced.
3. How my use of self with this case was influenced.
4. Questions that remain about my conduct of this case.

Index

Page number in **bold** refer to entries in the appendix.